The untold story of the men and women who made the greatest Scottish football managers

DEREK NIVEN

Corkerhill Press

Published in 2018 by Corkerhill Press

ISBN Paperback: 978-0-9935551-4-5
ebook: 978-0-9935551-5-2

A CIP catalogue copy of this book can be found at the British Library and at the National Library of Scotland.

Published with the help of Indie Authors World
www.indieauthorsworld.com

Acknowledgements

The author wishes to acknowledge the valued assistance of Indie Authors World partners Sinclair and Kim Macleod in the publishing of this book. Thanks also to my editor Gillian Murphy for her usual ardent efforts. A special thanks to my friend John Steele, who always takes a keen interest, whose footballing advice has been invaluable and thanks to Robin Dale, who initially encouraged me to 'kick on' with the idea of the 'Pride' series. Thanks to Jo Sherington, local history librarian at Dumbarton Library, for her help with Poor Law records and to ASGRA colleague Val Wilson for some valuable assistance with Busby ancestry.

As with my previous publications, *2084 The End of Days © 2016* and *Pride of the Lions © 2017*, gratitude goes to that great actor Sir Dirk Bogarde for the pseudonyms and to our old alumni Allan Glen's School for the superb education.

Finally, without the unswerving love, support and patience of my beautiful wife Linda this book would never have seen the light of day - never mind the end of days!

The best-laid schemes o' mice an' men,

Gang aft a-gley,

And leave us nought but grief and pain,

For promised joy.

Robert Burns, Scottish bard (1759-1796)

For James Peacock Cross

Contents

Foreword

By Kathleen Murdoch, wife of Bobby Murdoch, Lisbon Lion

I am pleased to write the foreword to Derek Niven's sequel to Pride of the Lions. Throughout my husband Bobby's career with Celtic and Middlesbrough, I did not have the pleasure to meet all the great managers in this book, but I certainly have good memories of the likes of Stein, Ferguson, Dalglish and Souness. Here are just a few.

Jock Stein

Many football fans may not know that Stein earned Bobby the nickname of 'Sam'. The Celtic team were training at Seamill, in North Ayrshire, and Stein laid out large paint pots for the players to train around. Bobby kept knocking the paint pots over to Stein's annoyance and the manager growled at Bobby calling him 'Sam Allison', a local Glasgow demolisher. When Stein kept complaining that Bobby was knocking over the equipment, Bobby retorted, "Aye boss, but we're no' playing paint pots on Saturday!" The nickname did not stick with everyone, but Jimmy Johnstone called Bobby 'Sam' for the rest of his life.

Alex Ferguson

At a function at Celtic Park, not long after Alex Ferguson received his knighthood, I approached him and asked, "Do I have to call you Sir Alex now?" He said, "Kathleen, you can call me what you like" and I replied, "Well, I'll just call you Fergie!" I always admired Alex because he never forgot his Glasgow roots or his old friends.

Graeme Souness

In the late 70s when Bobby was at Middlesbrough, he contacted Jock Stein to come down and look at Graeme Souness as a Scotland prospect. I was sitting in the 'Ladies' Lounge' at Ayresome Park and Stein popped in. I said to Jock, "Will I go and get Graeme for you?" Jock replied wryly, "No Kathleen that is not the way it is done!"

Kenny Dalglish

When Kenny Dalglish was just a young player at Celtic, during one of his first games, Bobby asked Kenny, "Are you nervous?" to which Kenny replied, "No." Bobby then exclaimed, "Well, you've got your boots on the wrong feet!" A few years later Bobby and I were guests at Kenny and his wife Marina's wedding. At that time Bobby was at Middlesbrough, but Jock Stein, who was also a guest, kept looking over and checking out what Bobby was eating. I wagged my finger at

Jock and said, "It's none of your business." Jock just laughed.

I hope you all enjoy reading Derek's book on the greatest Scottish managers.

Kathleen

Preface

As with my previous book, *Pride of the Lions: the untold story of the men and women who made the Lisbon Lions © Derek Niven 2017*, the reader may think this book is about the beautiful game of football. However, it is once again about fickle fate and destiny.

It researches the chance accumulation of fateful meetings and unions between men and women from the early 19th Century, which culminated in the procreation of a remarkable group of Scotsmen, who have written themselves into the history books through their exploits as football managers at the highest level of the game. It is about men and women who were born over half a century before the formation of the Scottish Football Association, which would give their descendants the start as professional footballers. These were people who were brought together by destiny, having no idea that one day their remarkable descendants would be immortalised over a century after their own births.

The author published *Pride of the Lions* in 2017 to celebrate the 50th anniversary of the Lisbon Lions and also mark the 130th anniversary of Celtic Football Club's formation. The publication of Pride of the Jocks in 2018 also marks the commemoration of the 60th anniversary of the terrible Munich Air Disaster in 1958 and the 50th anniversary of Manchester United winning the European Cup in 1968 – both synonymous with Sir Matt Busby.

However, as with Pride of the Lions, this book is not particularly a football book. The stories of these 16 remarkable Scottish managers and their careers have been written in their own autobiographies and by football journalists. This book is written from the perspective of their family histories. The author is a professional genealogist and member of ASGRA and the 'Pride' series is a sort of 'Wha D'ye Ken Ye Are?' of Scottish genealogies.

The reader may ask what brought a genealogist to want to write the family histories of the Lisbon Lions and Scottish managers. On the evening of 25 May 1967 my mother took me, aged eleven, up to my Gran McCue's high-rise flat in Pollokshaws in southwest Glasgow. My grandmother Annie was Protestant, but my grandfather Frank McCue and my uncle Jim were Catholic. As my mother chatted away to my grandmother, we 'men' sat enthralled watching the historic game unfold on the small Phillips black and white TV. Celtic became the first British team to win the European Cup and I went on to follow the Hoops. The following year I was again enthralled to watch, at my family home in Corkerhill, the reinvented Busby Babes of Manchester United win the European Cup, the first English side to do so. Similarly, I went on to follow United.

It was that support for Celtic dating back to 1967 that kindled within me the idea for Pride of the Lions and also my love of Manchester United going back to 1968 that was the spark for Pride of the Jocks. I had thought of doing the family histories of that magnificent 1968 United team, however, my forte is in Scottish ancestry and there was not enough Scottish history on show that evening at Wembley to justify my research into the players. Although, it must not be forgotten that Lisbon Lion medallist Charlie Gallagher of Celtic was the cousin of United medallist Paddy Crerand. They were both boys from the Gorbals with a shared Irish ancestry from County Donegal who went on to win the European Cup in successive years.

This book sets out to celebrate the legendary achievements of Busby, Shankly, Stein, Ferguson, Dalglish, et al, not from a footballing perspective but from a genealogical, familial, religious and social history perspective. It sets out to tell the story of these Scottish managers from the viewpoint of the direct ancestors who made that unique group of footballing leaders. It should also be noted that the greatest Scottish managers are selected from my own viewpoint. They are initially chosen from the fact that they all achieved their success in what is regarded as the modern era: the period when club football became global and clubs could enter into European and international competitions. I was born in 1956, which was about the time when the modern era really began, the same year the mighty Real Madrid won the first of their record breaking 12 European Cups.

This unfortunately precludes such great Scottish managers like Willie Maley, Jimmy McGrory and Bill Struth from having their chapters. Billy McNeill certainly merits a chapter in this book. Regrettably, McNeill was omitted as his family history has already been written in Pride of the Lions. Football fans will also argue about why their own favourite manager was omitted from this book, but then football has always been a game of opinions.

This book will also demonstrate that these managers were all from different sects of the Christian faith and that the Protestant / Catholic divide that persists in the West of Scotland was irrelevant to their quest for success. Jock Stein was once asked why he seemed to be signing too many Protestants for Celtic. Stein joked that he was signing up all the good Protestant footballers to ensure they did not end up at Ibrox, because he knew Rangers would not sign any good Catholic players.

This book serves to show that even in greatness we are, as we say in Scotland, "a' Jock Tamson's bairns". My own family history is a tale of poor, struggling agricultural labourers, coal miners and railway workers striving to achieve more than their working class existences afforded them. Within my own history are stories of heroism through two world wars, tales of illegitimacy, infant mortality and grinding poverty. The average reader may be able to associate their family history in the same vein.

Likewise, the genealogy of the greatest Scottish managers reveals a remarkably similar story of ordinary working class boys from predominantly poor backgrounds who went on to achieve something extraordinary. The book will reveal tales of family histories taking the descendancy from the Dickensian poorhouse to great riches within a few short generations.

In particular, Part 1 of the book will concentrate on the five legends that are Busby, Shankly, Stein, Ferguson and Dalglish. These five tough men of football were forged from the black coal and the wrought steel of the once burgeoning Scottish coal mining and Clyde shipbuilding industries.

The reader should be aware that it has not been possible to research every aspect of the lives of the ancestors of these managers and in the main the detailed research concentrates on their Scottish family history. Also, many of these men have now passed on to that great stadium in the firmament, but the book does not dwell on their passing. Thus, as with the Lisbon Lions in Pride of the Lions, the greatest Scottish managers will remain immortal.

Here are the greatest Scottish managers.

This is their amazing story.

Part 1

The Legends

Busby, Shankly, Stein, Ferguson and Dalglish

Chapter 1

Sir Matt Busby
Manchester United

Honours at Manchester United:
1 European Cup
5 English League 1 titles
2 FA Cups
5 FA Charity Shields

The young Matt Busby

When he was born, Matt's mother Nellie was told by the doctor: *"A footballer has come into this house today."* Alexander Matthew Busby was born in a humble 2-roomed pitman's cottage on 26 May 1909 at 28 Old Orbiston, Bellshill, Lanarkshire to father Alexander Busby and mother Helen Greer, aka Nellie.

Matt's father Alex was called up to serve in WWI and was killed by a sniper's bullet on 23 April 1917 at the Battle of Arras. Three of Matt's uncles were also killed in France with the Cameron Highlanders. Such was the loss in his family that Matt later stated by the end of the war that he and his grandfather Jimmy Greer were the only males left alive in the family. Future dramatic events in his life were also to challenge his own survival.

Matt's mother was left alone to raise Matt and his three sisters until she married Harry Mathie in 1919. Matt would often accompany his stepfather down the pits, but his true aspiration was to become a professional footballer. His mother might have quashed those dreams when she applied to emigrate - with Matt - to the United States in the late 1920s, but he was granted a reprieve by the nine-month processing time. Meanwhile, Matt got a full-time job as a collier and played football part-time for Stirlingshire side Denny Hibs. He had played only a few matches for Denny Hibs when he was signed up by Manchester City who were about to regain promotion to the First Division. Aged 18, Matt signed for City on a one-year contract worth £5 per week on 11 February 1928, with the proviso for him to leave at the end of the deal if he still wished to emigrate to the States.

In 1936 he signed for Liverpool and his playing career continued there until 1941. Bob Paisley had joined Liverpool from Bishop Auckland in 1939 and it was Matt who took him under his wing at Anfield. This led to a lifelong friendship between two of the most successful managers in English football history. WWII erupted soon after Paisley's arrival and with it came an end to Matt's playing days, apart from some guest appearances with various clubs. Like many of the Liverpool playing staff he signed on and enlisted in the King's Liverpool Regiment.

Busby the manager

During WWII, Busby was a football coach in the Army Physical Training Corps and the experience resulted in

Liverpool offering him the job of assistant to their manager George Kay. However, the experience also forged Busby's opinions about how football should be played and governed, and when it became clear that they differed from those of the Liverpool board, their chairman Billy McConnell allowed Busby to pursue alternate employment.

After Manchester United had tried to sign Busby from Manchester City in 1930, he became good friends with United's fixer, Louis Rocca, both members of the Manchester Catholic Sportsman's Club. United were in desperate need of a manager to take over after the war and a board meeting was called in December 1944. Knowing that Liverpool had already offered Busby a job, Rocca convinced the United board to "leave it to [him]" and immediately wrote a letter to Busby, addressed to his army regiment. The letter was vague, referring only to "a job", just in case it fell into the wrong hands, namely the Liverpool officials.

In February 1945, still in uniform, Busby appeared at Cornbrook Cold Storage, one of United chairman James W Gibson's businesses at Trafford Park to discuss the contents of Rocca's letter. Busby requested that he be directly involved in training, pick the team on match days and even buy and sell players without interference from the board. This was quite revolutionary in the professional game but United were desperate and agreed to Matt's terms. He signed on as manager of Manchester United in 1945, a post he was to hold onto through tragedy and triumph until 1971. During that early period Busby also managed the Great Britain team to the semi-finals of the 1948 Olympics in London. Thus began a stellar career, which brought Manchester United the greatest run of success in their history- until, of course, the Alex Ferguson era, but that is another chapter.

Busby brought five English League Division 1 titles, two FA Cups and five FA Charity Shields to Old Trafford. In the late 1950s Busby had been building a new young side which had earned the nickname the "Busby Babes", bringing through bright new stars such as Tommy Taylor, Harry Gregg, Duncan Edwards and Bobby Charlton. All that came to a crushing end on the night of 6 February 1958.

On the way home from a European Cup tie against Red Star Belgrade their plane crashed on the frozen runway at Munich-Riem Airport. Seven players and three club officials were among the 21 killed at the scene. Duncan Edwards died from his injuries two weeks later as the final death toll reached 23. Busby suffered multiple life threatening injuries and twice received the last rites, but he recovered and left hospital after nine weeks.

The author's friend Robin Dale, also a Manchester United fan, was devastated. Robin had been on National Service in the Royal Army Pay Corps based at Hounslow, Middlesex when, just five days earlier, on 1 February 1958, he got the chance to go along with another 63,500 fans to watch Arsenal play United. It was reported in the Daily Telegraph as one of the finest English league matches in history and the final score at Highbury was Arsenal 4 – Manchester United 5. Duncan Edwards, who was to be dead 3 weeks later, was imperious, but it was the last time the Busby Babes would play on British soil.

Busby miraculously went back to managing his beloved United. The Busby Babes had been decimated and Matt had to spend years rebuilding a new squad. However, it was to culminate in his greatest success - his dream of winning the European Cup. Celtic had become the first British team to win the European Cup in 1967 under his friend and footballing rival Jock Stein. Busby achieved it the following year at Wembley on 29 May 1968 when United crushed Eusébio's Benfica 4-1 with the likes of John Aston, Bobby Charlton, Paddy Crerand, Denis Law and the incomparable George Best. Busby was awarded the CBE in 1958 and he was knighted following the European Cup victory in 1968, before being made a Knight Commander of St Gregory by the Pope in 1972. A true great of world football, Sir Matt Busby deserves to be given the accolade of a legendary Scottish manager.

Matt's parents – Alexander Busby and Helen Greer

Alexander Busby was born on 2 November 1888 at Neilson's Rows, Orbiston in the district of Bothwell, Lanarkshire, to father Matthew Busby, a coal miner, and mother Catherine McPake. Alex was raised in the Protestant religion but converted to Roman Catholicism when he married his wife Nellie. Matt's mother was born Ellen Greer, aka Nellie, on 5 September 1891 at Netherburn, Dalserf, Lanarkshire, to father James Greer, a coal miner, and mother Bridget Crine.

Alexander Busby, 20, a coal miner, of 8 Old Orbiston, Bellshill, married Helen Greer, 17, a colliery worker, of 16 Old Orbiston, Bellshill, on Hogmanay, 31 December 1908, at the Holy Family Roman Catholic Church, Mossend. The wedding was conducted by Father Francis Cronin and the witnesses were Thomas and Bedelia Greer. Coincidentally, exactly 30 years later to the day, Billy McNeill's parents, also from Bellshill, married in Holy Family Church at Mossend on Hogmanay 1938. How many churches in Britain can boast in having conducted two marriages, each of which produced European Cup winners with two different teams?

Alex and Nellie had four known children, including son Matt (b. 26 May 1909, Old Orbiston, Bellshill), daughter Bedelia aka Beddie (b. ~1911) and two other daughters. In 1911 Alex Busby, 22, a coal driver below ground, resided at 28 Old Orbiston, Bellshill with wife Ellen, 19, son Matt, 1, and daughter Beddie, only 1 month old. Also living at Alex's home was his sister-in-law Beddie Greer, 21, a colliery pit-head worker, his father-in-law James Greer, 56, a coal hewer, and mother-in-law Bedelia Ann Greer, 58.

In 1914 Britain was thrust into the turmoil of the Great War and Alex Busby enlisted in the British army to fight the Kaiser's German army. Like many young coal miners of that time, the excitement of a fight in foreign climes away from the drudgery of the coal mines held great appeal. Little did they know that what they were to face in the muddy trenches of Flanders was to be far worse than any shift at the coal face. The Busby family was to face more than its fair share of tragedy on Flanders Field.

On 23 May 1915 Private S/20225 Alexander Busby, 7th Battalion Cameron Highlanders recorded an 'Informal Soldier's Will' in which he wrote in pencil: "WILL: In the event of my Death I give the whole my belongs [sic] to my Wife Mrs A Busby No.15 Old Orbiston Bellshill Lanarkshire Scotland." In the spring of 1916 the French had handed over the strategic town of Arras to Commonwealth forces and the system of tunnels upon which the town was built was used and developed in preparation for the major offensive planned for April 1917. Private Alexander Busby was killed by a sniper's bullet on 23 April 1917 during the Battle of Arras. He is commemorated on the Arras Memorial in the Pas de Calais Cemetery in France. His son Matt was aged seven and studying at primary school when his father was killed in action.

Matt also recorded that he lost three uncles in WWI, including his mother's brothers William and Thomas. William Greer was Private S/20227 and this suggests that William and Alex Busby enlisted in the Cameron Highlanders on the same day, being only two regimental numbers apart. At 7.30am on 1 July 1916 the dreadful Battle of the Somme commenced after a massive British bombardment. With 50,000 casualties on that first day it went down in infamy as the worst day in the history of the British Army. He survived that awful day but Private S/20227 William Greer 5th Cameron Highlanders was killed in action just over two weeks into the battle on 16 July 1916. He is commemorated on the Thiepval Memorial in the Somme region in France. On that same day of 16 July 1916 Private S/20226 William Mathie 5th Cameron Highlanders fell and he is also commemorated on the Thiepval Memorial. He was the brother of Matt's stepfather Harry Mathie.

A year later William Greer's brother Corporal 17137 Thomas Greer 189th Company Machine Gun Corps died of his wounds six days before Christmas on 19 December 1917. He is buried at Villers-Plouich Communal Cemetery south of Cambrai, Nord France. For his gallantry in battle Thomas was awarded the Military Medal. In his autobiography Matt wrote: *"First Uncle Willie, then my father, then Uncle Tommy. Every man was a miner and they all left widows."*

Alex Busby, William and Thomas Greer, Alex's best man, and William Mathie are all commemorated on the Bellshill War Memorial in front of Bellshill Academy on Main Street.

In 1919, left to bring up Matt and his three sisters, Nellie Busby married Harry Mathie. Probably still full of grief Nellie sought out a new life away from post-war Britain and in 1920 she filed papers to emigrate to the US. She had planned to take young Matt with her, which would certainly have altered the course of footballing history. However, the 9 month delay in the papers being processed allowed Matt to be signed by Manchester City and the rest is history.

Matt's paternal grandparents – Alexander Matthew Busby and Catherine McPake

Matt's paternal grandfather Alexander Busby, sometimes called Matthew, was born on 14 June 1859 at Glenhead, Dalziel, Lanarkshire to father Alexander Busby, a coal miner, and mother Mary Mundie. At that time the Busby family were Protestant, although Matt went on to be a very staunch Roman Catholic. In 1871, Alexander recorded as Matthew, 11, a scholar, resided at 2 Reid Street, Maryhill, Glasgow with his father Alexander Busby, 35, a printfield labourer, mother Mary, 37, sister Janet, 17, a printfield worker, and confusingly a brother called Alexander, aged four. Matt's grandmother Catherine McPake was born on 24 June 1861 at New Knowe, Carluke, Lanarkshire to father Bernard McPake, an ironstone miner, and mother Agnes Connelly.

Alexander Busby, 28, a coal miner, residing in Bellshill married Catherine McPake, 25, a domestic servant, of Law, Carluke on 9 December 1887 at Law. Alexander could not write and he signed with his 'x' mark as witnessed by Hugh and Thomas McPake, Catherine's brothers. The wedding was conducted by Rev W C Wagner, Church of Scotland; the best man was Alexander Dewar and the best maid was Maggie McPake, Catherine's sister. Alexander and Catherine had a known son Alexander, aka Alex, born on 2 November 1888 at Neilson's Rows, Orbiston in the district of Bothwell, Lanarkshire. Alexander Matthew Busby, a widowed coal miner, was still alive in 1909, although his wife Catherine Busby nee McPake was dead by then.

Matt's maternal grandparents – James Greer and Bridget Crine

Matt's maternal grandfather James Greer, aka Jimmy, was born around 1858 in Ireland to father James Greer, a coal miner, and mother Rose McStay. Matt's grandmother Bridget Crine (or Cryne), aka Bedelia Ann, was born around 1857 in Airdrie, Lanarkshire, to father Michael Cryne, a coal miner, and mother Bridget O'Hara. The Greers and Crynes were Roman Catholic and after the death of Matt's father Alex in WWI, Matt was brought up very much within his Greer grandparents' family circle and faith.

James Greer, 25, an iron miner, married Bridget Cryne, 26, a threadmill worker, both of 2 Newton Street, Paisley, Renfrewshire, on 29 December 1883 in St Mary's Roman Catholic Church, Paisley. The wedding was conducted by Fr

Arthur Bayaert, RC clergyman; the best man was Thomas Cryne, Bridget's brother, and the best maid was Mary McKennie. James and Bridget had seven known children; Mary (b. ~1882), James (b. ~1884, Old Monkland), Margaret (b. ~1887, Hoywood), Thomas (b. ~1888, Armadale), Bridget aka Beddie (b. ~1890, Dalserf), Ellen aka Nellie (b. 5 September 1891, Dalserf) and William.

In 1891, James Greer, 32, a coal miner, resided at Netherburn, Dalserf with wife Bridget, 34, children Mary, 9, a scholar, James, 7, a scholar, Margaret, 4, Thomas, 3, and Bridget, aged one. Also lodging at James's home was Peter Cryne, 18, a coal miner, and Patrick Cumming, 16, a coal miner. At the time Bridget was pregnant and daughter Ellen Greer was born on 5 September 1891 at Netherburn, Dalserf, Lanarkshire. In 1911, James Greer, 56, a coal hewer, resided at 28 Old Orbiston, Bellshill with wife Bedelia Ann, 58, daughter Beddie, 21, a colliery pithead worker, son-in-law Alex Busby, 22, a coal driver below ground, daughter Ellen, 19, and grandson Matt, aged one. James Greer was still alive in 1918 at the end of WWI, as his grandson Matt recorded that he and his grandfather James were the only two males left in the Busby and Greer lines.

Matt's great-grandparents – Alexander Busby and Mary Mundie

Matt's paternal great-grandfather Alexander Busby, aka Alex, was born around 1835 probably in Belfast, County Antrim, Ireland to father George Busby, a calico printer. By around 1844 the family had emigrated to Kilmarnock,

Ayrshire, but by 1851 the Busby family moved further north into Glasgow. This may have been due to the pressures of the massive influx of poor Irish families flooding into Ayrshire as a result of the Irish Potato Famine (1846-1852). In 1851, Alex, 15, a printfield worker, resided in Maryhill, Barony, Glasgow with his father George Busby, 45, a widowed calico printer, siblings Margaret, 19, a bonnet knitter, William, 17, a bleacher, Matthew, 12, a scholar, Jane, 11, a housemaid, and George, 7, a scholar. Matt's great-grandmother Mary Mundie (or Munday or Monday) was born around 1834 possibly in County Antrim, Ireland to father Bernard Mundie, a general labourer, and mother Margaret Kennedy.

Alexander Busby, a labourer, married Mary Mundie both residing in Maryhill on 2 October 1853 in the Barony of Glasgow as recorded in the OPRs as follows:-

OPR Marriages Barony 622/21/255

1853: 2 October: Alexander Busby labourer Maryhill & Mary Mundie residing there

Alex and Mary had three known children; Janet (b. ~1854, Maryhill), Alexander Matthew aka Matt (b. 4 June 1859, Glenhead, Dalziel) and Alexander (b. ~1867, Larkhall). In the 1850s and 60s Alex had a spell working as a coal miner in the Lanarkshire coalfields, however, by about 1870 he returned to Maryhill to work in the calico printing industry again. In 1871 Alexander Busby, 35, a printfield labourer, resided at 2 Reid Street, Maryhill, Glasgow with wife Mary, 37, children Janet, 17, a printfield worker, Matthew, 11, a scholar, and Alexander, 4.

The return to Glasgow may have been an ill-judged decision, as at that time one of the great killers of the Victorian era stalked the crowded slum tenements – tuberculosis, also known then as phthisis. Mary Busby nee Mundie, given as only 33, died on 5 July 1872 at 9 Kelvin Street, Maryhill of phthisis pulmonalis as registered by her husband Alexander Busby, a printfield worker. Alexander Busby, a coal miner, was still alive in 1887.

Tragedy once again struck the Busby family on 14 January 1893 when Matthew Busby, 51, a coal miner, and almost certainly Alex's younger brother, was killed in a mining accident. Matthew was working for the Summerlee & Mossend Iron and Steel Company on the 5th shift at the Orbiston Nos 1 and 2 pits when, at 9am that morning, he was crushed to death at the coal face after the roof and sides caved in.

Matt's great-grandparents – Bernard McPake and Agnes Connelly

Matt's other paternal great-grandfather Bernard McPake (or McPeake) was born around 1835 in Ireland to father Hugh McPake, a labourer, and mother Margaret McGrogan. His great-grandmother Agnes Connelly (or Conely) was probably born around 1842 in Ireland to father Bernard Connelly, a miner, and mother Catherine Burns. Bernard McPake, 25, a miner, residing in Carluke, Lanarkshire married Agnes Conely, 18, a house servant, residing in Braidwood, Lanarkshire, on 22 August 1860 at the Roman Catholic Chapel, Carluke. The wedding was conducted by Fr Mortimer Cassin, RC clergyman in Carluke; the best man was Robert Carrol and the best maid was Margaret Conely, Agnes's sister.

Bernard, an ironstone miner, and Agnes had three known children in Carluke; Hugh, Thomas and Catherine (b. 24 June 1861). Daughter Catherine was born on 24 June 1861 at New Knowe, Carluke, Lanarkshire. Bernard McPake, a coal miner, was dead by 1887, however, his wife Agnes McPake nee Conely was still alive at that time.

Matt's great-grandparents – James Greer and Rose McStay

Matt's maternal great-grandfather James Greer and great-grandmother Rose McStay were born about 1830 in Ireland and they had a known son James, aka Jimmy (b. ~1858) in Ireland. James Greer, a coal miner, was still alive in 1883, however, Rose Greer nee McStay was dead by that time.

Matt's great-grandparents – Michael Crine and Bridget O'Hara

Matt's other maternal great-grandfather Michael Crine (or Cryne) and great-grandmother Bridget O'Hara were also born about 1830 in Ireland and they possibly had three known children; Bridget, aka Bedelia Ann or Beddie (b. ~1857, Airdrie), Thomas and possibly Peter (b. ~1873, Johnstone). Michael Crine, a coal miner, was dead by 1883, however, Bridget Crine nee O'Hara was still alive at that time.

Matt's great-great-grandfather George Busby

Matt's great-great-grandfather George Busby was born about 1805 probably in Belfast, County Antrim, Ireland to father

James Busby, a shoemaker. Although George's first Irish wife has not been identified, they had six known children; Margaret (b. ~1832, Ireland), William (b. ~1834, Ireland), Alexander (b. ~1835, Ireland), Matthew (b. ~1839, Ireland), Jane (b. ~1840, Ireland) and George (b. ~1844, Kilmarnock). George, a calico printer, was widowed prior to 1851 by which time he was living and working in Maryhill, Glasgow.

In 1851, George Busby, 45, a widowed calico printer, resided in Maryhill, Barony, Glasgow with children Margaret, 19, a bonnet knitter, William, 17, a bleacher, Alex, 15, a printfield worker, Matthew, 12, a scholar, Jane, 11, a housemaid, and George, 7, a scholar. In 1861, George Busby, 52, a calico printer, resided at 34 Bridge Street, Maryhill, Glasgow with second wife Elizabeth Brown, 50, step-children Thomas Brown, 19, a printfield labourer, Elizabeth Brown, 16, a printfield tearer, and Maria Brown, 14, a printfield tearer. George's father James Busby, 70, also lived up the same tenement close at the time with second wife Jean, 45, and daughter Ellen, 19, a printfield worker.

Matt's other great-great-grandparents

Matt's great-great-grandfather Bernard Mundie and his great-great-grandmother Margaret Kennedy were born about 1810 in Ireland. Bernard, a general labourer, and wife Margaret had a known daughter Mary (b. ~1834) in Ireland. Bernard and Margaret were both dead by 1872.

Continuing on the paternal line, Matt's great-great-grandfather Hugh McPake (or McPeake) and his great-great-grandmother Margaret McGrogan were also born about 1810 in Ireland. Hugh, a labourer, and Margaret had a known son Bernard (b. ~1835) in Ireland. Hugh McPake, a labourer, and his wife Margaret McPake nee McGrogan were still alive in 1860.

Matt's great-great-grandfather Bernard Conely and his great-great-grandmother Catherine Burns were born about 1815 in Ireland. Bernard, a miner, and Catherine had two known daughters; Margaret and Agnes (b. ~1842) in Ireland. Bernard Conely, a miner, and his wife Catherine Conely nee Burns were still alive in 1860.

Matt's great-great-great-grandfather James Busby

Matt's great-great-great-grandfather James Busby, or Busbey, was born around 1776 as stated in Belfast, County Antrim. James Busby, a shoemaker in Belfast, was likely to have been married twice, although his first wife has not been identified. James Busby had a son George (b. ~1805) probably in Belfast. James emigrated to Scotland around the period of the devastating Irish Potato Famine (1846-52).

In 1851, James Busbey, 70, a shoemaker, resided at 1 Milton Street Row, Dunipace, Stirlingshire, with his second wife Jean, 45, a domestic, children Thomas, 15, a printworker, and Hellen, 13, a printworker. In 1861, James Busby, 85, a shoemaker, resided at 34 Bridge Street, Maryhill, Glasgow with wife Jane, 60, a shoemaker's wife, and daughter Ellen, 19, a printfield worker. His son George Busby and his family lived up the same close at that time. James Busby, given as 102 but more likely 92, a shoemaker married to Jane Walmsley, died on 21 May 1867 at 38 Bridge Street, Maryhill, Glasgow of senile decay as certified by Dr A Hay MD.

Chapter 2

Bill Shankly OBE
(Carlisle Utd, Grimsby Town, Workington, Huddersfield Town and Liverpool)

Honours at Liverpool:
1 EUFA Cup
3 English League 1 titles
1 English League 2 title
2 FA Cups
4 FA Charity Shields

The young Bill Shankly

Bill Shankly was born in the small Ayrshire coal mining village of Glenbuck, whose population in 1913, the year of his birth, was around 700. People born there would often move to find work in larger coal mines. As a result, Glenbuck became largely derelict and by the time Shankly's ghost writer John Roberts visited in 1976 there were only twelve houses left, including a cottage owned by Shankly's sister, Elizabeth, whom Roberts described as *"the last of the children of Glenbuck"*.

William Shankly was born on 2 September 1913 at Manse Place, Glenbuck, Ayrshire to father John Shankly, a letter carrier, and mother Barbara Gray Blyth. Shankly was the ninth child and the youngest boy of 10. Although he was known as Bill throughout his football career, his name in the family was Willie.

Shankly wrote that times were hard during his upbringing and hunger was a prevailing condition, especially during the winter months. He admitted that he and his friends used to steal vegetables from nearby farms; bread, biscuits and fruit from carters' wagons and bags of coal from the pits. Shankly admitted the act was wrong but said it was *"devilment more than badness"* and the root cause was hunger, but he insisted that they learned from their mistakes and became better people. Discipline at both home and school was strict but Shankly said it was character building. His favourite subject was geography and he played football as often as possible in the school playground.

After Shankly, 14, left school in 1928, he worked at a local mine alongside his brother Bob. He described the life of a miner and mentioned many of the problems such as the sheer hard work, the rats, the difficulties of eating and drinking at the coal face, but above all the filth, and said: *"We were never really clean. It was unbelievable how we survived. Going home to wash in a tub was the biggest thing. The first time I was in a bath was when I was 15!"*

He worked in the mines for two years until the pit closed and he faced unemployment. Shankly played football as often as possible and sometimes went to Glasgow to watch both Celtic and Rangers, sharing his allegiance and ignoring the sectarianism that divided Glasgow. Shankly's village team was the Glenbuck Cherrypickers, a name probably derived from the 11th Hussars, the "Cherry Pickers", but Shankly said: *"The club was near extinction when I had a trial and I never actually played for them."*

Shankly, aged 18, then played part of the 1931–32 season for Cronberry Eglinton in the Cumnock & District League. Although Shankly had less than one full season at Cronberry, he acknowledged his debt to Scottish Junior Football where he "learnt a lot", mainly by listening to older players, especially his brothers. Shankly developed his skills to the point that he was quickly signed by Carlisle United. He always believed optimistically that he was destined to become a professional footballer.

Shankly the manager

Shankly's playing career was interrupted by his service in the Royal Air Force during WWII. He became a manager after he retired from playing in 1949, returning to manage Carlisle United. He later managed Grimsby Town, Workington and Huddersfield Town before moving to become Liverpool manager in December 1959, where his career took off. Shankly took charge of Liverpool when they were languishing in the Second Division and rebuilt the team into a major force in English and European football. At Liverpool, Shankly was noted for his personality and wit. His most famous quotation is probably one that is most often misquoted. *"Some people believe football is a matter of life and death, I am very disappointed with that attitude. I can assure you it is much more important than that."*

He led Liverpool to the Second Division Championship to gain promotion to the First Division in 1962, before going on to win three First Division Championships, two FA Cups, four Charity Shields and one UEFA Cup. It had also been his dream to take Liverpool on to win the European Cup, after seeing his friends and rivals Jock Stein and Matt Busby achieve this.

Shankly announced his surprise retirement from football a few weeks after Liverpool had won the 1974 FA Cup Final, having managed the club for 15 years and was succeeded by his long-time assistant Bob Paisley. Shankly's retirement was surprisingly announced at a press conference called by Liverpool on 12 July 1974. Chairman, John Smith, stated: *"It is with great regret that I as chairman of Liverpool Football Club have to inform you that Mr Shankly has intimated that he wishes to retire from active participation in league football. The board has with extreme reluctance accepted his decision. I would like to at this stage place on record the board's great appreciation of Mr Shankly's magnificent achievements over the period of his managership."* Bill Shankly led the Liverpool team out for the last time at Wembley for the 1974 FA Charity Shield.

Bill's parents – John Shankly and Barbara Gray Blyth

Bill's father John Shankly was born on 23 January 1873 in Douglas, Lanarkshire, to father Alexander Shankly, a journeyman tailor, and mother Jessie, aka Janet, Brown Wight. In 1881 John, 8, a scholar, resided at the Cross, Douglas with his father Alexander Shankly, 33, a tailor, mother, Jessie, 32, siblings Jessie, 11, a scholar, Alexander, 9, a scholar, Sarah, 6, a scholar, William, 4, Marion, 3, and baby Andrew, aged one. After leaving school John became a tailor like his father Alexander.

Bill's mother Barbara Gray Blyth was born on 19 April 1877 in the mining village of Glenbuck, Muirkirk, Ayrshire, to father James Blyth, a coal miner, and mother Janet Fleming. In 1881, Barbara, aged 3, resided at Glenbuck with father James Blyth, 40, a stone miner, mother Janet, 34, siblings John, 15, a general labourer, Robert, 11, a scholar, Marion, 7, a scholar, and baby Hannah, aged one. In 1891, Barbara, 13, resided at Blyth's Buildings, Glenbuck with her parents and siblings. By this time Barbara had left school and she went into domestic service, which took her east across the Ayrshire moors to work in Douglas, Lanarkshire where she fell in love with John Shankly.

John Shankly, 23, a journeyman tailor, married Barbara Gray Blyth, 18, a domestic servant, both residing in Douglas, Lanarkshire, on 3 April 1896 in Douglas. The wedding was conducted by Rev William Smith, Free Church of Scotland minister at Douglas; the best man was Alexander Shankly, John's brother, and the best maid was Hannah Blyth, Barbara's sister. Around 1903, John and Barbara eventually moved from Douglas to Glenbuck in Ayrshire where they raised their 10 children. John and Barbara, lived in one of the Auchenstilloch Cottages in Glenbuck with their children; five boys and five girls. Included in their children were; Alexander aka Sandy (b. ~1897, Douglas), Janet (b. ~1900, Douglas), James aka Jimmy (b. ~1902, Douglas), John (b. ~1904, Glenbuck), Elizabeth (b. ~1907, Glenbuck), Isobel (b. ~1908, Glenbuck), Robert aka Bob (b. ~1910, Glenbuck), William aka Willie or Bill (b. 2 September 1913, Glenbuck) and two other daughters.

In 1911, John Shankly, 38, a tailor and auxiliary postman, resided at Manse Row, Glenbuck with wife Barbara, 34, children Alexander, 14, a pit bottomer's assistant, Janet, 11, at school, James, 9, at school, John, 7, at school, Elizabeth, 4, Isobel, 3, and baby Robert, aged one. Son William Shankly was born on 2 September 1913 at Manse Place, Glenbuck, Ayrshire. Bill's father was a postman and letter carrier and also a tailor of handmade suits like his father before him, but, despite the football pedigree in his family, John Shankly did not play the game himself. His five sons went on to distinguish themselves in the beautiful game.

All five Shankly brothers played professional football and Bill wrote that *"once, when we were all at our peaks, we could have beaten any five brothers in the world"*. His brothers were Alex, known as 'Sandy' by the family, who played for Ayr United and Clyde; Jimmy, who played for various clubs including Sheffield United and Southend United; John, who played for Portsmouth and Luton Town; and Bob, who played for Alloa Athletic and Falkirk. Bob Shankly also became a successful manager, guiding Dundee to victory in the Scottish Division 1 championship in 1962 and the semi-finals of the European Cup the following year. Their maternal uncles, Robert and William Blyth, Barbara's brothers, were also professional players and both became club directors at Portsmouth and Carlisle United respectively.

Bill's paternal grandparents – Alexander Shankly and Janet Brown Wight

Bill's paternal grandfather Alexander Shankly, aka Alex, was born around 1847 in Lanark, the county town of Lanarkshire, to father Alexander Shankly, a shoemaker, and mother Jane Dunlop. It is likely that Alexander was raised in the strict Free Church of Scotland, which had been established just four years before his birth, in 1843, after breaking away from the Established Church, in what was called the 'Great Schism'. In 1851, Alexander, 4, resided at 1 Greenside Lane, Lanark with father Alexander Shankly, 28, a shoemaker, mother Jane, 26, a shoemaker's wife, and baby sister Catherine, 10 months old.

Bill's paternal grandmother Janet Brown Wight, aka Jessie or Jess, was born around 1849, also in Lanark, to father John Brown Wight, a tailor, and mother Sarah Neil, a cotton weaver, and it appears Janet was born illegitimately. Alexander Shankly, 18, married Jess Brown Wight, 18, both residing in Lanark, on 9 August 1865. The wedding was conducted by Rev Thomas Stark, minister of Lanark Free Church of Scotland; the best man was William Harvey and the best maid was Sophie McGarvy.

Alex and Jessie had seven known children; Janet aka Jessie (b. ~1870, Lanark), Alexander (b. ~1872, Douglas), John (b. 23 January 1873, Douglas), Sarah (b. ~1875, Douglas), William (b. ~1877, Douglas), Marion (b. ~1878, Douglas) and Andrew (b. ~1880, Douglas). Son John Shankly was born on 23 January 1873 in Douglas, Lanarkshire. In 1881, Alexander Shankly, 33, a tailor, resided at the Cross, Douglas with wife Jessie, 32, children Jessie, 11, a scholar, Alexander, 9, a scholar, John, 8, a scholar, Sarah, 6, a scholar, William, 4, Marion, 3, and Andrew, aged one. Alexander Shankly, a journeyman tailor, and his wife Jessie Brown Wight were still alive in 1896.

Bill's maternal grandparents – James Blyth and Janet Fleming

Bill's maternal grandfather James Blyth was born around 1840 in Muirkirk, Ayrshire to father John Blyth, a coal miner, and mother Marion McLellan. In 1851, James, 11, probably still at school, resided at Wellwood Row, Muirkirk with his parents and siblings. Bill's grandmother Janet Fleming was born around 1847 in Tynron, Dumfriesshire to father Robert Fleming, a shepherd, and mother Barbara Gray. After leaving school Janet went into domestic service in Muirkirk where she met young coal miner James Blyth.

James Blyth, 24, a coal miner, residing in Muirkirk married Janet Fleming, 17, a domestic servant, of High Boig, New Cumnock, on 16 December 1864 at High Boig farm. The wedding was conducted by Rev George Anderson of New Cumnock Free Church of Scotland; the witnesses were John Blyth and Robert Fleming, the fathers of the betrothed. James and Janet had six known children in Glenbuck; John (b. ~1866), Robert (b. ~1870), Marion (b. ~1874), Barbara (b. 19 April 1877), Hannah (b. ~1880) and William J (b. ~1883). Daughter Barbara Gray Blyth was born on 19 April 1877 in the mining village of Glenbuck, Muirkirk.

In 1881, James Blyth, 40, a stone miner, resided at Glenbuck with wife Janet, 34, children John, 15, a general labourer, Robert, 11, a scholar, Marion, 7, a scholar, Barbara, 3, and Hannah, age one. In 1891, James Blyth, 51, a coal miner, resided at Blyth's Buildings, Glenbuck with wife Janet, 44, children Robert, 21, a coal miner, Marion, 17, assistant Cooperative storekeeper, Barbara, 13, Hannah, 11, a scholar, and William J, 8.

By the turn of the 20th century James had given up coal mining, set some money aside, and moved to Douglas, Lanarkshire, to start his own business as a drapery trader. In 1901, James Blyth, 61, a trader in drapery, resided at Pathhead, Douglas with wife Janet, 54, daughter Hannah, 21, a domestic servant at home, son William, 18, a coal miner, and granddaughter Janet, 3. James and Janet's sons Robert and William Blyth went on to become professional footballers and both were club directors at Portsmouth and Carlisle United respectively. In fact, the Blyth brothers being older than the five Shankly boys were probably the progenitors of what became a family footballing dynasty.

Bill's paternal great-grandparents – Alexander Shankly and Jane Dunlop

Bill's paternal great-grandfather Alexander Shankly (or Shankley or Shanklie) was born around 1823 in Pettinain, Lanarkshire, and his great-grandmother Jane Dunlop was born around 1825 in the county town of Lanark. It is likely that they were married in the Lanark Free Church of Scotland around 1845, shortly after its formation. Alexander, a shoemaker, and Jane had two known children in Lanark; Alexander (b. ~1847) and Catherine (b. ~1850). In 1851, Alexander Shankly, 28, a shoemaker, resided at 1 Greenside Lane, Lanark with wife Jane, 26, a shoemaker's wife, son Alexander, 4, and daughter Catherine, 10 months old. Their cottage was next door to Grace Lyon's inn on Greenside Lane. Alexander Shankly, a shoemaker, was still alive in 1865, however, his wife Jane Shankly nee Dunlop was dead by then.

Bill's paternal great-grandparents – John Brown Wight and Sarah Neil

Bill's other paternal great-grandfather John Brown Wight and his great-grandmother Sarah Neil were born around 1825 probably in the county town of Lanark. John worked as a tailor in Lanark and Sarah Neil was a young cotton weaver. Sarah fell pregnant and it appears that she gave birth illegitimately to a daughter Janet Brown Wight (b. ~1849) in Lanark. It was common practice for a woman to name their child after the putative father, thus Sarah named Janet, aka Jessie or Jess, after the errant tailor John Brown Wight. The likelihood is that John and Sarah would have been called before the Kirk Session to be rebuked for their fornication, however, it appears that they never married each other. John Brown Wight, a tailor, and Sarah Neil, a cotton weaver, were still alive in 1865.

Bill's maternal great-grandparents – John Blyth and Marion McLellan

Bill's maternal great-grandfather John Blyth, or Blythe, was born around 1811 in Kirkconnel, Dumfriesshire and his great-grandmother Marion McLellan was born around 1813 in Caerlaverock, Dumfriesshire. John, a coal miner, and Marion had 7 known children in Muirkirk, Ayrshire; John (b. ~1835), Robert (b. ~1838), James (b. ~1840), David (b.

~1842), Marion (b. ~1844), Hannah (b. ~1846) and George (b. ~1849). In 1851, John Blyth, 40, a coal miner, resided at Wellwood Row, Muirkirk with wife Marion, 38, children John, 16, a coal miner, Robert, 13, a coal miner, James, 11, Marion, 7, David, 9, Hannah, 5, and George, 2. John Blyth, a coal miner, and his wife Marion Blyth nee McLellan were still alive in 1864.

Bill's maternal great-grandparents – Robert Fleming and Barbara Gray

Bill's other maternal great-grandfather Robert Fleming and his great-grandmother Barbara Gray were born around 1820 possibly in Tynron, Dumfriesshire. Robert, a shepherd, and Barbara had a known daughter Janet (b. ~1847) in Tynron. Robert Fleming, a shepherd, was still alive in 1864 and, in fact, Robert stood as a witness at his daughter's marriage on 16 December 1864 at High Boig, Muirkirk in Ayrshire. Robert's wife Barbara Fleming nee Gray was dead by 1864.

Chapter 3

Jock Stein CBE
(Dunfermline, Hibernian, Celtic, Leeds and Scotland)

Honours at Celtic:
1 European Cup
10 Scottish League 1 titles
8 Scottish Cups
6 Scottish League Cups

The young Jock Stein

Jock Stein was undoubtedly the greatest and most successful football manager to grace the Scottish game. To his friends he was known as John but in the game he was always 'Big Jock'. John Stein was born on 5 October 1922 at 339 Glasgow Road, Hamilton, Lanarkshire, to father George Stein, a coal miner, and mother Jane McKay Armstrong.

After leaving school Stein worked as a coal miner while playing football part-time for junior side Blantyre Victoria and then he moved to Scottish League side Albion Rovers. He became a full-time professional footballer with Welsh club Llanelli Town, but returned to Scotland with Celtic in 1951. He enjoyed some success with Celtic, winning the Coronation Cup in 1953 and a Scottish league and cup double in 1954. Ankle injuries forced Stein to retire from playing football in 1957.

Stein the manager

Celtic appointed Stein to coach their reserves after he retired as a player. Stein's ambition was to manage his beloved Celtic, however, the chairman at Parkhead, Sir Robert Kelly, made it clear to Stein that he had gone as far as he could with Celtic. Stein was a Protestant and Kelly felt that this would not be accepted by the Celtic faithful. How wrong this would prove to be. Stein started his managerial career in 1960 with Dunfermline, where he won the Scottish Cup in 1961. After a brief spell at Hibernian, the Celtic board relented and Stein returned to Celtic as manager in March 1965, following in the footsteps of Jimmy McGrory. In 13 years at Celtic, Stein won an unprecedented 10 Scottish league championships, including the famous "nine-in-a-row" run between 1966 and 1974, eight Scottish Cups and six Scottish League Cups.

Stein became renowned for his tactical and strategic nuance at Celtic and was a real hands-on man-manager, which was not always appreciated by some of his players. It was known for Big Jock to prowl the pubs of Uddingston on a Friday night to ensure his star player Jimmy Johnstone was fit to play on Saturday. Stein's respect for Johnstone's skill was immense and he once reported in the Daily Telegraph when asked what he regarded as his greatest achievement. Stein famously stated: *"I would like to be remembered for keeping the wee man, Jimmy Johnstone, in the game five years longer than he might have been. That is my greatest achievement."*

However, undoubtedly his greatest success was in becoming the first manager of a British side to win the European Cup with Celtic in 1967. In choosing that legendary Celtic team for the 25 May 1967 to play Inter Milan in the Estádio Nacional in Lisbon, Stein had developed a strategy of using attacking full backs Jim Craig and Tommy Gemmell to thwart the ultra-defensive Italians. After Alessandro Mazzola's seventh minute penalty goal, the defensive Internazionale thought they had put the game beyond lowly Celtic's reach. It was even reported that the Inter players were celebrating in the dressing room at half time.

However, Stein stuck to his tactics of using the overlaps down the wings, which paid off in the second half. After a cut back from Craig, a fearsome 63rd minute strike by marauding defender Gemmell scored the equaliser. This was followed in the 83rd minute when a Bobby Murdoch shot was deftly guided into the Italian net by Stevie Chalmers to seal the victory for Celtic. On that balmy night in Portugal, Stein had given birth to the legend of the Lisbon Lions – a group of working class 'Bhoys' all born within 30 miles of Parkhead. This feat will never be repeated in the modern game of world football.

After a brief stint with Leeds United, Stein managed the Scottish national side from 1978 until his death in 1985 during the World Cup qualifier in Cardiff, between Wales and Scotland. Although Scotland gained the required draw thanks to a Davie Cooper equaliser, the game became secondary when news got out that Jock had collapsed with a heart attack. Alex Ferguson was Stein's assistant-manager on that fateful evening and on the cusp of going on to greatness himself. Ferguson had immense respect for Stein and big Jock's ethos had a great influence on Ferguson's own man-management style. Stein's life was succinctly summed up in Lisbon in 1967 by his great friend Bill Shankly of Liverpool, who stated: *"John – you're immortal!"*

Jock's parents – George Stein and Jane McKay Armstrong

Jock's father George Stein was born on 15 April 1887 at Thomson's Buildings, Blantyre, Lanarkshire, to father John Stein, a coal miner, and mother Margaret Johnston. After leaving school George followed his father down the mines. Jock's mother Jane McKay Armstrong was born on 5 December 1890 at 109 Castle Street, Townhead, Glasgow, to father John Armstrong, a flesher's assistant, and mother Georgina McKay Scouller. The tenement at 109 Castle Street was later replaced by the Glasgow Royal Infirmary. After leaving school Jane became a stationer's book sewer and, given her location in Glasgow, this was likely to have been with the expanding Collins publishing house on nearby Cathedral Street.

George Stein, 29, a coal miner, of 339 Glasgow Road, Hamilton, married Jane McKay Armstrong, 25, a stationer's book sewer, of 11 Dunchattan Street, Dennistoun, Glasgow, on 10 November 1916, during WWI, at Jane's home. The wedding was conducted by Rev Alexander Cross, minister of Bluevale Parish Church; the best man was Robert Kilgour and the best maid was Georgina Armstrong, Jane's sister. The wedding took place eight days before the end of the devastating Battle of the Somme in France and Flanders. When it drew to a close for the winter on 18 November 1916 the British and Allies had sustained over half a million casualties. George Stein's protected occupation as a coal miner probably saved him from the slaughter in the trenches.

George and Jane had five known children in Hamilton; at 13 Greenfield Road, Georgina Scouller (b. 16 March 1917); and at 339 Glasgow Road, Margaret Johnstone (b. 21 January 1920, likely to have died in infancy), John aka Jock (b. 5 October 1922), Jessie Scott Armstrong (b. 12 July 1925) and Margaret Dempsey Johnstone (b. 10 November 1927). It is a matter of conjecture but Jock Stein was a sort of father figure to Jimmy Johnstone, one of his most errant but gifted players. Possibly the fact that Stein's own grandmother was a Johnstone and his sisters carried the surname made him more sympathetic to wee Jinky.

Jock's paternal grandparents – John Stein and Margaret Johnston

Jock's paternal grandfather was born as John Steven on 17 February 1856 at West Maryston, Old Monkland, Lanarkshire, to father Adam Steven, a coal miner, and mother Marion Sneddon. It can be seen here the surname Stein is actually a local Scottish dialectic form of Steven. In 1861, John, 6, resided at Crawford's Land, West Maryston with his parents and siblings. After any schooling John followed his father Adam down into the bowels of the Lanarkshire coalfields. At that time pits were opening up at a rapid rate to meet the demands of the fast growing Industrial Revolution.

Jock's paternal grandmother Margaret Johnston, or Johnstone, was born around 1858 in Old Monkland, Lanarkshire, to father Robert Johnston, a coal miner, and mother Margaret Dempsey and after any schooling Margaret became an agricultural labourer. John Stein, 21, who signed with his 'x' mark, married Margaret Johnston, 19, who signed with her 'x' mark, both of West Maryston, on 13 July 1877 at Swing Bridge, Old Monkland. The wedding was conducted by Rev Alexander T Scott, minister at Bargeddie Church of Scotland; the best man was George Scobbie and the best maid was Mary Aitken. Other witnesses present were William and Elizabeth Johnston, likely to be Margaret's brother and sister.

John and Margaret had three known children; Margaret (b. ~1880, Old Monkland), Adam (b. ~1881, Old Monkland, d. 7 March 1882) and George (b. 31 April 1887, Blantyre). In 1881, John Stein, 25, a coal miner, resided at No.3 Drumpark & Garbraid, Bargeddie, Old Monkland with wife Margaret, 23, a coal miner's wife, and daughter Margaret, aged one. Residing next door at No.4 Drumpark & Gairbraid was John's older brother Robert Stein, 32, a coal miner, with his wife Mary, 29, and their children Adam, 11, James, 9, Elizabeth, 7, Robert, 5, Marion, 3, and John, aged one.

At the time Margaret was pregnant with son Adam and he was born around November 1881. Adam Stein, only 5 months old, died on 7 March 1882 at West Maryston, Old Monkland of meningitis, which he fought for four days. Son George Stein was born on 15 April 1887 at Thomson's Buildings, Blantyre, Lanarkshire.

Eight years after his own father was killed down the pits John Stein, only 34, a coal miner, of Thomson's Buildings, Stonefield, Blantyre, was also killed at work at 2.30am on

17 May 1890 at Lettrick Pit, Cambuslang and he was *"killed instantaneously by a fall of stones from the roof of said pit while at work"*. In a Register of Corrected Entries signed by Robert Wilson, Procurator Fiscal's Office, Hamilton on 26 May 1890, the cause of death was confirmed as per John's death certificate stating that the accident occurred on: *"1890 May 17th in the Ell Coal Seam at Lettrick Colliery, Cambuslang at a working place known as Paton's Mine 400 yards from the pit bottom"*. John's widow Margaret Stein nee Johnstone was still alive in 1916 during the ravages of WWI.

Jock's maternal grandparents – John Armstrong and Georgina McKay Scouller

Jock's maternal grandfather John Armstrong was born around 1863 possibly in Glasgow, Lanarkshire, to father James Armstrong, an iron roller, and mother Jane Powell. John went on to become a flesher's assistant, an old term for a butcher's helper. Jock's grandmother Georgina Scouller was also born around 1863 again possibly in Glasgow to father John Scouller, a house painter, and mother Jane McKay. After schooling Georgina took a job as a sewing machinist in a clothing factory.

John Armstrong, 24, a flesher's salesman, of 238 Garngadhill, Garngad, Glasgow, married Georgina Scouller, 24, a sewing machinist, of 134 Garngadhill, Garngad, Glasgow, on 25 November 1887 at 69 Garngad Road, Glasgow. The wedding was conducted by Rev Thomas Somerville, minister of Blackfriars Church of Scotland; the best man was John Scouller, Georgina's brother, and the best maid was Christina Johnston.

In the 19th and early 20th centuries the Garngad was still known by its original historic name, derived from the Gaelic word 'garn' meaning rough ground surrounding the Gad burn. It was home to a high proportion of Irish Catholic immigrants who gained employment in the gas, chemical, iron, steel and railway works in the adjacent districts of Provan, St Rollox and Springburn. However, during the era of the Great Depression in the 1920s, which earned Glasgow its 'No Mean City' label of slums, drunkenness, violence and razor gangs, the reputation of the Garngad became deeply tarnished. It landed itself with the Glasgow rhyming slang moniker of 'The Garngad - the Good and the Bad'.

The City Fathers decided in 1942 to rename the area Royston, after the legendary Rob Roy MacGregor, who once lived there in the early 18th century. This was followed by a programme of slum clearance and housing redevelopment in the early 1950s. However, the historic name of the Garngad still fondly persists with the local inhabitants today and the local public house on Royston Road retains the name - 'The Garngad'. Jock Stein probably had little idea of an ancestral link to the Garngad, but two of Celtic's famous sons were 'Garngad Bhoys' – Jimmy McGrory and Lisbon Lion Stevie Chalmers.

John and Georgina had two known daughters in Glasgow; Jane McKay (b. 5 December 1890) and Georgina. Daughter Jane McKay Armstrong was born on 5 December 1890 at 109 Castle Street, Townhead. John Armstrong, who later became an engineer's machinist, and wife Georgina Armstrong nee Scouller were still alive and living in Dennistoun in 1916, during WWI.

Jock's paternal great-grandparents – Adam Steven and Marion Sneddon

Jock's paternal great-grandfather Adam Steven, or Stein, was born around 1827 to father Adam Steven, a coal miner, and mother Mary Robertson in the Barony of Glasgow. His great-grandmother Marion Sneddon, or Snedden, was born around 1826 to father Robert Sneddon, a coal miner, and mother Janet Russell also in the Barony of Glasgow. Adam Steven, a collier, married Marion Sneddon on 20 March 1846 in Cambuslang, Lanarkshire as recorded in the OPRs as follows:-

> *OPR Ref: 627/2/209 Cambuslang Marriage Register 1846*
> *[Enrolled] February 14: Adam Steven, Collier, and Marion Snedden, both in this Parish: [Married] 20 March*

Adam, a coal miner, and Marion had seven known children; George (b. ~1847, Cambuslang), Robert (b. ~1849, Rutherglen), Adam (b. ~1851, Old Monkland), possible twins John and Agnes (b. 17 February 1856, West Maryston), William (b. ~1859, West Maryston) and Marion (b. ~1860, West Maryston). In 1851, Adam Stein, 24, a pithead ventilator, resided at Commonhead, Crosshill, Old Monkland with wife Marion, 25, and their three sons George, 4, Robert, 2, and baby Adam, 5 months old. Also living with Adam was his older Glasgow-born brother John Stein, 34, a widowed coal miner, and his son John, aged three. Son John was born on 17 February 1856 at West Maryston, Old Monkland, Lanarkshire.

In 1861, Adam Steven, 35, a coal miner, resided at Crawford's Land, West Maryston, Old Monkland with wife Marion, 36, children George, 14, a coal miner, Robert, 12, a coal miner, Adam, 8, a scholar, John and Agnes, 6, possible twins, William, 2, and Marion, eight months old. However, by 1866 Adam was a widower. Marion Steven nee Sneddon, aged 40, died on 7 November 1866 at West Maryston of exhaustion.

Adam Stein, 40, a coal miner, still of West Maryston married second wife Eliza Hynds, 37, residing in New Dundyvan, Coatbridge, on 30 April 1867 at Sneddon's Land, Coatbridge. The wedding was conducted by Rev P Cameron Black, minister of Old Monkland Parish Church; the witnesses were John Raeside and William Thomson. Adam Stein, a coal miner, was still alive in 1877, however, five years later tragedy struck. Adam Steven, 56, a coal miner, was killed at work about 11.30am on 22 August 1882 at Neatherhouse Pit, Baillieston by a "fall of stones and coal upon his body while working" and he suffered an "instantaneous death".

Jock's paternal great-grandparents – Robert Johnston and Margaret Dempsey

Jock's other paternal great-grandfather Robert Johnston and his great-grandmother Margaret Dempsey (or Demstey) were born around 1825 possibly in Old Monkland, Lanarkshire. Robert and Margaret had three known children probably in Old Monkland; William, Elizabeth and Margaret (b. ~1858). Robert Johnston, a coal miner, was dead by 1877, although his wife Margaret Johnston nee Dempsey was still alive.

Jock's maternal great-grandparents – James Armstrong and Jane Powell

Jock's maternal great-grandfather James Armstrong and his great-grandmother Jane Powell were born around 1835 possibly in Glasgow, Lanarkshire. James, an iron roller, and Jane had a known son John (b. ~1863) possibly in Glasgow. James Armstrong, an iron roller, and his wife Jane Armstrong nee Powell were still alive in 1887.

Jock's maternal great-grandparents – John Scouller and Jane McKay

Jock's other maternal great-grandfather John Scouller and his great-grandmother Jane McKay were born around 1835 possibly in Glasgow, Lanarkshire. John, a house painter, and Jane had a known son John and a daughter Georgina (b. ~1863) possibly in Glasgow. John Scouller, a house painter, was dead by 1887, however, his wife Jane Scouller nee McKay was still alive.

Jock's paternal great-great-grandparents – Adam Steven and Mary Robertson

Jock's paternal great-great-grandfather Adam Steven, or Stein, and his great-great-grandmother Mary Robertson were born around 1790 both possibly in the Barony of Glasgow. Adam and Mary had three known children in Barony; John (b. ~1817), Adam (b. ~1827) and Mary (b. ~1831). Adam Steven, a collier, and his wife Mary Steven nee Robertson were both dead by 1867.

Jock's paternal great-great-grandparents – Robert Sneddon and Janet Russell

Jock's other paternal great-great-grandfather Robert Sneddon, or Snedden, and his great-great-grandmother Janet Russell were born around 1800 both possibly in the Barony of Glasgow. Robert and Janet had a known daughter Marion (b. ~1826) in Barony. Robert Sneddon, a coal miner, was dead by 1866, however, his wife Janet Sneddon nee Russell was still alive at that time.

Chapter 4

Sir Alex Ferguson
(East Stirlingshire, Saint Mirren, Aberdeen, Manchester United and Scotland)

Honours at Manchester United:

2 European Cups
1 EUFA Cup Winners Cup
1 EUFA Super Cup
1 FIFA Club World Cup
1 Intercontinental Cup
13 English League 1 titles
5 FA Cups
4 FA League Cups
10 FA Charity Shields

The young Alex Ferguson

Ferguson was born at his grandmother's home at 357 Shieldhall Road, Govan, Glasgow on Hogmanay 1941, during the dark days of WWII. Alexander Chapman Ferguson was born on 31 December 1941 to father Alexander Beaton Ferguson, a plater's helper in the Clyde shipbuilding industry, and mother Elizabeth Hardie. He was initially raised at 6 Broomloan Road, Govan in the shadow of Ibrox Stadium and was an avid Rangers supporter, dreaming of one day playing at Ibrox. He grew up in a tenement at 667 Govan Road, Glasgow, where he lived with his parents and his younger brother Martin. Ferguson attended Broomloan Road Primary School and Govan High School. After leaving school Ferguson followed his father as an apprentice shipwright into the Govan shipyards.

He began his football career with Harmony Row Boys Club in Govan, before moving to Drumchapel Amateurs. Ferguson's senior career began as an amateur with Queen's Park, where he made his debut aged 16, moving to St Johnstone in 1960. At St Johnstone he was unable to command a regular place. However, St Johnstone's failure to sign a forward led its manager to select Ferguson for a 1963 match against Rangers, in which he scored a hat-trick. In 1964, Dunfermline Athletic signed him and Ferguson became a full-time professional. The 1965–66 season saw Ferguson notch up 45 goals in 51 games for Dunfermline. Along with Joe McBride of Celtic, he was equal top goal scorer in the Scottish League with 31 goals.

In 1967, he joined Rangers for a record transfer fee between two Scottish clubs. He performed well in Europe during his two seasons with the club. However, Ferguson was blamed for a goal conceded in the 1969 Scottish Cup Final, in a match in which he was assigned to mark Celtic captain, Billy McNeill, and he was subsequently forced to play for the club's reserves. According to his brother Martin, Ferguson was so upset by the experience that he threw his losers' medal away. It was claimed that he suffered discrimination at Rangers after his marriage to Roman Catholic wife Cathy Holding, but Ferguson stated that Rangers knew of his wife's religion when he joined the club. He left Rangers reluctantly due to the fall-out from his cup final mistake.

Nottingham Forest wanted to sign Ferguson, but Cathy was not keen, so he went to Falkirk instead. He remained at Brockville for four years and he was promoted to player-coach, but when John Prentice became manager, he removed Ferguson's coaching responsibilities. Ferguson responded by requesting a transfer and moved to Ayr United, finishing his playing career in 1974.

Ferguson the manager

Alex Ferguson is the greatest manager ever to grace British football and he has been rated in the top ten of EUFA all-time greats. It will be a long time before Scotland produces a manager of his calibre again. His record is unparalleled in world football, having won just about every honour available in Scotland, England, Europe and world club levels. The press and the fans nicknamed him 'Fergie', a name that became synonymous with other Ferguson-related metaphors such as the "New Firm", the "siege mentality", the "Class of 92", the "hairdryer treatment" and "Fergie time".

After spells at East Stirlingshire and St Mirren, where he won the Scottish First Division in 1976-77, Ferguson joined Aberdeen as manager in June 1978. He replaced Billy McNeill who was offered the chance to return to Celtic. Although Aberdeen were one of Scotland's major clubs they had won the league only once before in 1955. Fergie took Aberdeen to heights of success that they could only have dreamed of with players such as Jim Leighton, Willie Miller, Alex McLeish and Gordon Strachan. Under his management Aberdeen won three Scottish Premier League titles, four

Scottish Cups, one Scottish League Cup and a Drybrough Cup. This was capped by Aberdeen's historic 2-1 victory over the mighty Real Madrid on 11 May 1983 in the European Cup Winners' Cup and a European Super Cup win over European Champions Hamburger SV in December 1983.

Ferguson was assistant manager for the Scottish national side during qualifying for the 1986 World Cup. Tragically, manager Jock Stein, who Ferguson held in high esteem, had collapsed and died in Cardiff on 10 September 1985, when Scotland qualified for a play-off against Australia. Ferguson agreed to take charge of the Scottish national side against the Australians and subsequently at the World Cup. To allow him to fulfil his international duties he appointed Archie Knox as co-manager at Aberdeen. However, after Scotland failed to progress past the group stages of the World Cup, Ferguson stepped down as national team manager on 15 June 1986.

Ferguson was appointed Manchester United manager on 6 November 1986, but the success he had achieved at Aberdeen appeared to elude him for three long years. In 1989-90, following an early season run of six defeats and two draws, a banner declared: *"Three years of excuses and it's still crap.... ta-ra Fergie."* He later described December 1989 as *"the darkest period he had ever suffered in the game"* as United ended the decade just outside the relegation zone. Ferguson later revealed that the board of directors had assured him that they were not considering his dismissal.

The 1990 FA cup win is often cited as the match that saved Ferguson's Old Trafford career. United went on to win the FA Cup, beating Crystal Palace 1–0 in the final replay, giving Ferguson his first major trophy as United manager. Fergie's stellar career at Old Trafford took off and in the next 13 years he steered United to an unprecedented 13 Premier League titles, five FA Cups, four English League Cups, ten FA Charity Shields, two EUFA Champions Leagues, two EUFA Cup Winners' Cups, one EUFA Super Cup, one Intercontinental Cup and a FIFA Club World Cup.

Just days after winning the FA Cup final, United travelled to Barcelona, the setting for the 1999 Champions League final. Ferguson contemplated his team selection against Bayern Munich. Suspensions to Paul Scholes and Roy Keane ruled both players out. David Beckham was positioned in centre midfield, Ryan Giggs was moved to the right wing and Jesper Blomqvist started on the left. Fergie felt these changes would prevent the Germans from playing narrow. However, United conceded in the first six minutes from Mario Basler's free kick.

Teddy Sheringham substituted Blomqvist and he equalised from a corner in the first minute of additional time. Steve McClaren told Ferguson they needed to get the team organised for extra time. Fergie famously replied: *"Steve, this game isn't finished!"* Three minutes into added time Ole Gunnar Solskjær scored an unbelievable winner, which completed an unprecedented treble for United. Ferguson, interviewed moments after, exclaimed: *"I can't believe it. Football, bloody hell. But they never gave in and that's what won it!"*

Ferguson was knighted by the Queen in 1999 for his services to football. On 8 May 2013, Sir Alex Ferguson announced that he was to retire as manager at the end of the season, but would remain at the club as director and club ambassador.

The Guardian announced it was the "end of an era", while UEFA president Michel Platini said that Ferguson was "a true visionary". Prime Minister David Cameron described Ferguson as a "remarkable man in British football".

Alex's parents – Alexander Beaton Ferguson and Elizabeth Hardie

Alex's father Alexander Beaton Ferguson was born on 29 October 1912 at 107 Main Street, Renton, Dunbartonshire to father John Ferguson, a plater's helper, and mother Janet Montgomery Beaton, aka Jenny. The family later moved to 357 Shieldhall Road, Govan and Alexander went to work as a ship plater's helper in the world famous Govan shipyards. It was in Govan during WWII that he met Elizabeth Hardie, almost 10 years his junior. Alex's mother Elizabeth Hardie was born on 17 January 1922 at 13 Albert Street, Govan, Glasgow to father Archibald Hardie, a tramcar conductor, and mother Susan Mansell. After leaving school Elizabeth got a job as a rubber factory worker, possibly in the nearby Dunlop rubber works at Inchinnan.

Alexander Beaton Ferguson, 28, a ship plater's helper, of 357 Shieldhall Road, Govan, married Elizabeth Hardie, 19, a rubber factory worker, of 12 Neptune Street, Govan, on 27 June 1941 at 639 Govan Road, Glasgow. The wedding was conducted by Rev Thomas Notman, minister of Govan St Mary's Church of Scotland; the best man was John Ferguson, Alex's brother, of 5 Dunvegan Street, and the best maid was Mary Agnes Hardie, Elizabeth's sister, of 12 Neptune Street, Govan. Just five days previously Hitler launched Operation

Barbarossa on the Eastern Front which brought Stalin's Soviet Union into the war. Alex and Elizabeth had two known sons; Alexander and Martin.

Alex's paternal grandparents – John Ferguson and Janet Montgomery Beaton

Alex's paternal grandfather John Ferguson was born on 26 September 1880 at 129 High Street, Dumbarton, to father Robert Ferguson, a journeyman riveter, and mother Catherine Mulholland. In 1891, John, 10, a scholar, resided at 101 High Street, Dumbarton with his parents and siblings. After schooling John went to work in the Dumbarton shipyards, probably with the main shipbuilder in the area, Denny & Co. Within five years John was an orphan as his parents Robert and Catherine both succumbed to the dreaded tuberculosis.

Alex's paternal grandmother Janet Montgomery Beaton, aka Jenny, was born around 1890 possibly in Renton, Dunbartonshire, to father Alexander Beaton, 29, a hammerman, and mother Isabella Fairley. John Ferguson, a ship plater's helper, of 16 West Bridgend, Dumbarton married Jenny Montgomery Beaton, 22, a printfield worker, of 82 Main Street, Renton, on 23 August 1912 at the Public Hall, Renton. The wedding was conducted by Rev A H Macpherson, officiating minister, United Free Church of Scotland; the best man was George Ferguson, John's brother, and the best maid was Mary McGregor.

Son Alexander Beaton Ferguson was born just nine weeks later on 29 October 1912 at 107 Main Street, Renton, Dunbartonshire. John Ferguson, a ship plater's helper, was dead by 1941, however, his wife, who had remarried and was now Janet Miller previously Ferguson nee Beaton was still alive at that time during WWII.

Alex's maternal grandparents – Archibald Hardie and Susan Mansell

Alex's maternal grandfather Archibald Hardie was born around 1896 probably in Glasgow to father Robert Hardie, an iron moulder, and mother Mary McFarlane. After leaving school Archie became a tramcar conductor at Govan Depot in the once extensive Glasgow tramway system. His grandmother Susan Mansell was born around 1899 also probably in Glasgow to father Thomas James Mansell, a quay labourer, and mother Winifred Shields. After schooling Susan got a job as a laundress. Archibald Hardie, 23, a tramcar conductor, of 123 Crookston Street, now named Carnoustie Street, Glasgow, married Susan Mansell, 19, a laundress, at St Saviour's Roman Catholic Chapel, Govan, on 26 September 1919. The wedding was conducted by Fr William Daly; the best man was Alexander Hardie, Archie's brother, and the best maid was Annie Mansell, Susan's sister.

Archie and Susan had two known daughters in Govan; Elizabeth and Mary Agnes. Daughter Elizabeth Hardie was born on 17 January 1922 at 13 Albert Street, Govan. However, within a couple of years Archie and Susan's marriage irretrievably broke down and unusually for a Roman Catholic marriage it ended in divorce in 1925. Archibald Hardie, a tramcar conductor, and Susan Hardie nee Mansell were both still alive in 1941.

Alex's paternal great-grandparents – Robert Ferguson and Catherine Mulholland

Alex's paternal great-grandfather Robert Ferguson was born illegitimately on 6 September 1854 in Dumbarton, Dunbartonshire, to father Robert Ferguson, a sawyer, and mother Anne Scullion. Robert was baptised on 8 September by Fr R A Wilson in St Patrick's RC Church in Dumbarton as recorded in the Catholic Parish Registers as follows:-

CPR Births Dumbarton, St Patrick's

1854: September 8th: Robert natural son of Robert Ferguson & Anne Scullion, born 6th instant, sponsor Sarah Irvine: [Priest] R A Wilson

Robert's father Robert was dead by 1861. In 1861, Robert Ferguson, 7, a scholar, lodged at the home of a widowed Irishwoman named Margaret, 78, at 90 High Street, Dumbarton, with his mother Anna Scullion, 36, a widowed washerwoman, and his brother John, 3. In 1871, Robert Ferguson, 16, a riveter, resided at 152 High Street, Dumbarton with his mother Ann Scullion, 50, still a washerwoman, and his brother John, 12, a rivet heater.

Alex's paternal great-grandmother Catherine Mulholland was born around 1859, probably in Dumbarton, to father John Mulholland, a quarryman, and mother Agnes Hendry. Robert Ferguson, a journeyman riveter, married Catherine Mulholland on 11 July in Dumbarton. Robert and Catherine had five known children in Dumbarton; John (b. 26 September 1880), Mary (b. ~1883), Catherine (b. ~1887), George (b. ~1889) and Patrick (b. ~1891). Son John Ferguson was born on 26 September 1880 at 129 High Street, Dumbarton.

In 1891, Robert Ferguson, 35, a riveter, resided at 101 High Street, Dumbarton, with his wife Catherine, 31, children John, 10, a scholar, Mary, 8, a scholar, Catherine, 4, George, 2, and Patrick, less than a month old. Just three years later that terrible Victorian killer tuberculosis (or phthisis) stalked the Ferguson household. Catherine Ferguson, only 35, died on 11 March 1894 at 107 High Street, Dumbarton, of phthisis pulmonalis as certified by Dr William Little MD PhD (Camb).

Tragically, Robert also contracted tuberculosis the following year in 1895 and unable to work he was admitted to the Dumbarton Combination Poorhouse at Townend Road. The workhouse was erected on the northern outskirts of the town in 1862 and an infirmary block for up to 60 patients, unfortunately named the lunacy wards, was added in 1866. Robert Ferguson, 40, a pauper and formerly a riveter, died on 16 May 1896 at the Dumbarton Combination Poorhouse of phthisis pulmonalis as certified by Dr James Wilson LFP&S (Glasgow) and the death was registered by John Henderson, lunatic warder. Robert Ferguson died a pauper in the poorhouse, but within a few short generations his descendant would become an illustrious multi-millionaire.

The records of the Dumbarton Poorhouse are scant for this period, however, the following report by the Commissioner for the lunacy wards probably confirms the death of Robert Ferguson, but also gives an insight into the conditions faced by inmates in the infirmary block.

> *At the Quarterly Meeting of the Dumbarton Combination Poor House Committee held within the Board Room of the Poor House the 13th August*

1896....A report by Dr John Sibbald, Commissioner in Lunacy, respecting the Condition of the Lunatic Wards of the House and the Inmates thereby, dated the 13th June last, was laid before the Meeting. This Report was also ordered to be engrossed in the Minutes. It is as follows viz:- "Lunatic Wards, Dumbarton Poorhouse, 13th June 1896. There are 29 men and 31 women in the wards as patients at this date. Since 13th January, the date of last visit, one man has been admitted and one man has died. The patients were found in a satisfactory condition. They are suitably clothed, and their food is good and plentiful. All are employed in useful and healthy work except those whose bodily condition makes them unfit. The recommendation in the preceding entry as to the improvement of the bathing and water closet arrangements are here repeated. The books and registers were found regularly and correctly kept." [signed] John Sibbald, Commissioner in Lunacy.

Alex's paternal great-grandparents – Alexander Beaton and Isabella Fairley

Alex's other paternal great-grandfather Alexander Beaton, and also the likely progenitor of Alex Ferguson's first name, and his great-grandmother Isabella Fairley were born around 1860, possibly in Dunbartonshire. Alexander, a hammerman, and Isabella had a known daughter Janet Montgomery Beaton, aka Jenny (b. ~1890) possibly in Renton, Dunbartonshire. Alexander Beaton, a hammerman, was still alive in 1912, however, his wife Isabella Beaton nee Fairley was dead by that time.

Alex's maternal great-grandparents – Robert Hardie and Mary McFarlane

Alex's maternal great-grandfather Robert Hardie and his great-grandmother Mary McFarlane were born around 1870 possibly in Glasgow. Robert, an iron moulder, and Mary had two known sons; Archibald, aka Archie (b. ~1896) and Alexander. Robert Hardie, an iron moulder, was dead by 1919, however, his wife, who had remarried, Mary McDonald previously Hardie nee McFarlane was still alive at that time.

Alex's maternal great-grandparents – Thomas James Mansell and Winifred Shields

Alex's other maternal great-grandfather Thomas James Mansell and his great-grandmother Winifred Shields were born around 1870 possibly in Glasgow. Thomas, a quay labourer, and Winifred had two known daughters; Susan (b. ~1899) and Annie. Thomas James Mansell, a quay labourer, was dead by 1919, however, his wife, Winifred Mansell nee Shields was still alive at that time.

Alex's paternal great-great-grandparents – Robert Ferguson and Anne Scullion

Alex's paternal great-great-grandfather Robert Ferguson was born around 1820, possibly in Ireland, although this has not been fully confirmed. Alex's great-great-grandmother Agnes Scullion, aka Ann or Anna, was born about 1825 in Ireland and she almost certainly emigrated to Dumbarton to escape the ravages of the Irish Potato Famine (1846-52). Robert Ferguson, a sawyer, co-habited with his common law wife Ann Scullion and they had two known illegitimate sons in Dumbarton; Robert (b. 6 September 1854) and John (b. 20 June 1858). Son Robert was born on 6 September 1854 and baptised on 8 September by Fr R A Wilson in St Patrick's Roman Catholic Church, Dumbarton, as recorded in the Catholic Parish Registers. Son John Ferguson was born on 20 June 1858 in High Street, Dumbarton.

However, Robert Ferguson was dead before 1861 and Ann was left a widow to raise two young boys and she took in people's washing to make ends meet. In 1861, Anna Scullion, 36, a washerwoman, lodged at the home of a widowed Irishwoman named Margaret, 78, at 90 High Street, Dumbarton, with her sons Robert Ferguson, 7, a scholar, and John, 3. Also lodging there was Elizabeth Scullion, 28, a washerwoman, likely to be Ann's younger sister. In 1871, Ann Scullion, 50, still a washerwoman, resided at 152 High Street, Dumbarton, with sons Robert Ferguson, 16, a riveter, and John, 12, a rivet heater. Ann Scullion was dead by 1896.

Alex's paternal great-great-grandparents – John Mulholland and Agnes Hendry

Alex's other paternal great-great-grandfather John Mulholland and his great-great-grandmother Agnes Hendry were born about 1830, probably in Ireland. John, a quarryman probably at Dumbuck Quarry, near Dumbarton, and Agnes had a known daughter Catherine (b. ~ 1859) possibly in Dumbarton. John Mulholland, a quarryman, was dead by 1894, however, his wife Agnes Mulholland nee Hendry was still alive at that time.

Chapter 5

Sir Kenny Dalglish

(Liverpool, Blackburn Rovers, Newcastle United and Celtic)

Honours at Liverpool:
3 English League 1 titles
2 FA Cups
1 English League Cup
1 Super Cup
4 FA Charity Shields

The young Kenny Dalglish

As this book was going to press, Kenny Dalglish was knighted in the Queen's 2018 birthday honours list. Kenneth Mathieson Dalglish was born on 4 March 1951 at 76 Ardenlea Street, Dalmarnock, Glasgow, to father William Borland Dalglish, a motor vehicle fitter, and mother Catherine Rice Munro. Ardenlea Street was made famous on BBC's '*Who Do You Think You Are?*' in 2005. Jeremy Paxman discovered his widowed great-grandmother Mary McKay lived there in the late 19th century in a slum tenement and was refused poor relief after she was discovered with an illegitimate child.

The Dalglish family moved from the run-down east end and Kenny was raised in Milton on the north side of Glasgow. Aged

15, the family moved to Flat 25 at 5 Broomloan Court, Ibrox, in a high-rise block overlooking Ibrox Stadium and Kenny grew up supporting Rangers. Dalglish attended Milton Bank Primary School and High Possil Secondary School, where he won the inter-schools five-a-side competition. On advice from Vic Davidson, ex-Celtic Quality Street boy, Celtic manager Jock Stein sent assistant Sean Fallon to visit Dalglish at his parents' home. On hearing that Fallon was at the door, Dalglish hurried to remove the Rangers posters from his bedroom walls. Fallon kept his irate wife and kids waiting for three hours downstairs in his car, but he got Kenny to sign a provisional contract with Celtic in May 1967.

Dalglish was loaned out to Cumbernauld United and he worked as an apprentice joiner. He began his senior career with Celtic in 1971, going on to win four Scottish league championships, four Scottish Cups and one Scottish League Cup. Jimmy Johnstone was rightly voted the greatest Celtic player of all time, but in the author's opinion, Dalglish was the greatest player he ever saw playing at Parkhead in the early 70s. In 1977, Liverpool manager Bob Paisley paid a British transfer record bringing Dalglish to Anfield.

His years at Liverpool were among the club's most successful, where he won six English league championships, two FA Cups, four League Cups, seven FA Charity Shields, three European Cups and one UEFA Super Cup. Dalglish won the Ballon d'Or Silver Award in 1983, the PFA Players' Player of the Year in 1983, and the FWA Footballer of the Year in 1979 and 1983. For his achievements he was nicknamed 'King Kenny' and in 2006 he topped a Liverpool fans' poll of '100 Players Who Shook the Kop'.

Dalglish the manager

Dalglish became player-manager of Liverpool in 1985, winning a further three First Divisions, two FA Cups and four FA Charity Shields. He was manager of Liverpool during the Hillsborough disaster in Sheffield on 15 April 1989. The disaster claimed 94 lives on the day, with the final death toll reaching 96. Dalglish attended many funerals of the victims and his presence in the aftermath of the disaster has been described as *"colossal and heroic"*. He resigned from Liverpool in 1991. Eight months later Dalglish made a return to management with Blackburn Rovers, leading them from the Second Division to win the Premier League in 1995. Soon afterwards he stepped down as Blackburn manager to become Director of Football, before leaving in 1996.

In January 1997 Dalglish took over as manager at Newcastle United. Newcastle finished runners-up in both the Premier League and FA Cup during his first season. Dalglish was appointed Director of Football at Celtic in 1999, and later manager, where he won the Scottish League Cup, before an acrimonious departure the following year. In January 2011, Dalglish was appointed Liverpool's caretaker manager, after the dismissal of Roy Hodgson, becoming permanent in May 2011. Despite winning the League Cup which earned them a place in the Europa League and reaching the FA Cup Final, Liverpool could only finish eighth in the league and Dalglish was dismissed in May 2012. In October 2013, Dalglish returned to Anfield as a non-executive director. On 3 May 2017, in recognition of his contribution Anfield's Centenary Stand was renamed the Kenny Dalglish Stand.

Kenny's parents William Borland Dalglish and Catherine Rice Munro

William Borland Dalglish was born on 1 November 1915, during WWI, at 14 Millerfield Road, Bridgeton, Glasgow, to father David Dalglish, an engineer's patternmaker, and mother Mary Ann Borland. Almost eight weeks later, Catherine Rice Munro was born on 23 December 1915 at 166 Stanley Street, Kinning Park, Glasgow, to father John Ewing Munro, a packing case maker, and mother Catherine Rice. After schooling William became a motor lorry driver and Catherine worked in a creamery.

A few months into WWII, William Borland Dalglish, 24, a motor lorry driver, of 141 Hamilton Road, Rutherglen, married Catherine Rice Munro, 24, a creamery worker, of 11 Nimmo Drive, Glasgow, on 2 February 1940 at McGregor Memorial Church of Scotland. The wedding was conducted by Rev Duncan Macpherson, minister of McGregor Memorial; the best man was William Paterson and the best maid was Helen Mathieson Dalglish Paterson.

William enlisted as a Private in the Argyll & Sutherland Highlanders and was away on war service when daughter Catherine was born. Argyll battalions were attached to the British Expeditionary Force and in late May 1940 were fighting a rear-guard action with the 51st Highland Division during the retreat to Dunkirk. Daughter Catherine Dalglish was born on 31 May 1940 at the Rottenrow Maternity Hospital, Glasgow.

After WWII ended, William returned to Glasgow and worked as a motor vehicle fitter. Son Kenneth Mathieson Dalglish was born on 4 March 1951 at 76 Ardenlea Street,

Dalmarnock, Glasgow. The family moved to the Milton district and then to Govan in the mid-1960s.

Kenny's paternal grandparents David Dalglish and Mary Ann Borland

Kenny's paternal grandfather David Dalglish was born on 27 June 1888 at 600 Dalmarnock Road, Bridgeton, Glasgow, to father Alexander Dalglish, a machinist, and mother Helen Matheson. David, a Protestant, was born about a mile away from Parkhead where grandson Kenny's club Celtic would erect their new stadium. About four weeks before David's birth Celtic played their first game in May 1888, beating Rangers 5-2 in a friendly match. When he left school David became an engineer's patternmaker. His grandmother Mary Ann Borland was born on 16 June 1890 at 16 Farie Street in the Royal Burgh of Rutherglen to father William Borland, a coal miner, and mother Matilda Malcolm. After schooling Mary Ann became a power-loom weaver.

David Dalglish, 24, an engineer's patternmaker, of 707 Dalmarnock Road, Bridgeton, Glasgow, married Mary Ann Borland, 22, a power-loom weaver, of 69 High Street, Rutherglen, on 12 July 1912. The wedding was conducted by Rev George Simpson Yuille BD, minister of Rutherglen Parish Church; the best man was Kenneth Matheson Dalglish, David's brother, and the best maid was Elizabeth Borland, Mary Ann's sister. The wedding would not have been short of music as the Orange Flute Bands would have been parading through Glasgow on the 12th of July.

David and Mary Ann had five known children at 14 Millerfield Road, Bridgeton; Alexander (b. 6 September 1912), William Borland (b. 2 June 1914, d. 5 June 1914, premature birth), William Borland (b. 1 November 1915), Helen Mathieson (b. 29 November 1918) and David (b. 12 April 1923). Son William Borland Dalglish was born on 1 November 1915, during WWI, at 14 Millerfield Road, Bridgeton. David Dalglish, only 44, an engineer's patternmaker still at 14 Millerfield Road, Glasgow, died on 21 January 1933 at Strathclyde Pavilion, Silverdale Street, Glasgow of angina pectoris as seen after death by Dr J Whiteford MB ChB. In a Register of Corrected Entries dated 3 March 1933, the sudden death was confirmed by Robert MacDonald, Procurator Fiscal Depute as follows: *"David Dalglish, 44 years, male. On 21st January 1933 at 1h 15m AM in the pavilion of the Strathclyde Football Club, Silverdale Street, Glasgow. Cause of death: angina pectoris."* After David's death his wife remarried a second husband surnamed Dobbin. Mary Ann Dobbin, previously Dalglish, nee Borland was still alive in 1940.

Kenny's maternal grandparents - John Ewing Munro and Catherine Rice

Kenny's maternal grandfather John Ewing Munro was born on 20 June 1871 in Glasgow to father Donald Munro, a baker, and mother Marion Gibb. His grandmother Catherine Rice was born around 1876 probably in Old Monkland, Lanarkshire, to father William Rice, a lamplighter, and mother Mary Ann Doyle. John Ewing Munro, 32, a packing case maker, married Catherine Rice, 27, a handkerchief folder, both at 3 Green Street, Calton, Glasgow, on 18 September 1903 at 1 Broompark Circus, Dennistoun. The wedding was conducted by Rev William Chalmers Smith, minister of Calton Parish Church; the best man was William Gemmell and the best maid was Mary Richardson.

Daughter Catherine Rice Munro was born on 23 December 1915, during WWI, at 166 Stanley Street, Kinning Park, Glasgow. John Ewing Munro, a packing case maker, was dead by 1940, however, his wife who had remarried, Catherine Richardson, previously Munro, nee Rice was still alive then.

Kenny's paternal great-grandparents - Alexander Dalglish and Helen Matheson

Kenny's paternal great-grandfather Alexander Dalglish was born around 1849, probably in Glasgow, to father David Dalglish, a coal miner, and mother Margaret Gray. His great-grandmother Helen Matheson was born around 1854, probably in Glasgow, to father Kenneth Matheson, a coal miner, and mother Janet McIntyre. Alexander Dalglish, 26, a sewing machine work mechanic, of 166 Dalmarnock Road, Bridgeton, Glasgow, married Helen Matheson, 21, a cotton power-loom weaver, of 20 Scott Street, Bridgeton, on 5 March 1875. The wedding was conducted by Rev John Campbell, minister of Newhall Church; the best man was James Dalglish, Alexander's brother, and the best maid was Catherine Matheson, Helen's sister.

Alexander and Helen had two known sons in Bridgeton; Kenneth Matheson and David (b. 27 June 1888). Son David

Dalglish was born on 27 June 1888 at 600 Dalmarnock Road, Bridgeton, Glasgow. Alexander Dalglish, a boring machinist, and wife Helen Dalglish nee Matheson were still alive in Bridgeton in 1912.

Kenny's paternal great-grandparents - William Borland and Matilda Malcolm

Kenny's other paternal great-grandfather William Borland was born around 1856 probably in Rutherglen, Lanarkshire, to father Andrew Borland, a colliery redsman, and mother Martha Tippon. His great-grandmother Matilda Malcolm was born around 1860, probably in Rutherglen, to father John Malcolm, a coal miner, and mother Elizabeth Laughlan. William Borland, 23, a colliery redsman, of 14 Mill Street, Rutherglen married Matilda Malcolm, 19, who signed with her 'x' mark, of 11 Farie Street, Rutherglen on 18 July 1879. The wedding was conducted by Rev Thomas A Patrick, minister of the Congregational Church; the best man was Joseph Ray and the best maid was Elizabeth Borland, Matilda's sister.

William and Matilda had three known children in Rutherglen; Elizabeth (b. 3 November 1881), Mary Ann (b. 16 June 1890) and William (b. 14 February 1893). Daughter Mary Ann Borland was born on 16 June 1890 at 16 Farie Street, Rutherglen. William Borland, a coal miner, and wife Matilda Borland nee Malcolm were still alive in Rutherglen in 1912.

Kenny's maternal great-grandparents - Donald Munro and Marion Gibb

Kenny's maternal great-grandfather Donald Munro and great-grandmother Marion Gibb were born around 1835 and they were married on 31 October 1867 in Kirkintilloch, Dunbartonshire. Donald, a baker, and Marion had three known children in Glasgow; Alexander (b. 15 May 1869), John Ewing (b. 20 June 1871) and Marion Gibb (b. 28 May 1873). Donald Munro, a baker, was still alive in 1903, however, wife Marion Munro nee Gibb was dead by then.

Kenny's maternal great-grandparents - William Rice and Mary Ann Doyle

Kenny's maternal great-grandfather William Rice and great-grandmother Mary Ann Doyle were born around 1845 probably in Inverness-shire. William and Mary Ann had three known children; William Andrew (b. 1 December 1873, Bracadale, Inverness), Catherine (b. ~1876, Old Monkland) and Margaret (b. 17 May 1881, Old Monkland). William Rice, a lamplighter, and wife Mary Ann Rice nee Doyle were both still alive in Rutherglen in 1903.

Kenny's great-great-grandparents

Kenny's paternal great-great-grandfather David Dalglish and great-great-grandmother Margaret Gray were born around 1820. They had two known sons probably in Glasgow; Alexander (b. ~1849) and James. David Dalglish, a coal miner, and wife Margaret Dalglish nee Gray were still alive in 1875.

Kenny's other paternal great-great-grandfather Kenneth Matheson and great-great-grandmother Janet McIntyre were born around 1825. Kenneth and Janet had two known daughters probably in Glasgow; Helen (b. ~1854) and Catherine. Kenneth Matheson, a coal miner, was dead by 1875, although, his wife Janet Matheson nee McIntyre was still alive then.

Kenny's other paternal great-great-grandfather Andrew Borland and great-great-grandmother Martha Tippon were born around 1825. Andrew and Martha had two known children probably in Rutherglen; William (b. ~1856) and Elizabeth. Andrew Borland, a colliery redsman, and his wife Martha Tippon were both still alive in 1879.

Kenny's other paternal great-great-grandfather John Malcolm and great-great-grandmother Elizabeth Laughlan were born around 1830. John and Elizabeth had a daughter Matilda (b. ~1860) probably in Rutherglen. John Malcolm, a coal miner, and his wife, who remarried, Elizabeth Perrie, previously Malcolm, nee Laughlan were dead by 1879.

Part 2

The Other Great Scottish Managers

Chapter 6

Willie Waddell
(Kilmarnock and Rangers)

Honours at Kilmarnock:
1 Scottish League 1 title
Honours at Rangers:
1 European Cup Winners' Cup
1 Scottish League Cup

The young Willie Waddell

William Tweedie Orr Waddell was born on 7 March 1921 at Orr's Buildings, Forth, Lanarkshire, to father Walter Young Waddell, a coal miner, and mother Grace Clarkston Stark Orr. In his youth Waddell played at amateur level for Forth Wanderers and Strathclyde. Waddell played professionally for Rangers in a career spanning both sides of WWII. He made his debut at aged 17 in a friendly match against Arsenal and went on to win four League titles and two Scottish Cups. His rhyming moniker at Ibrox was 'Deedle-Doddle'. Waddell earned 18 caps for Scotland, scoring six times.

Waddell the manager

Waddell became manager of Kilmarnock in 1957. In what was their most prosperous era, the club achieved four runners-up placings in the league under his guidance between 1960 and 1964 and reached three cup finals. Kilmarnock's efforts were finally rewarded when the club won their only league championship in 1964–65. On leaving Kilmarnock in 1965 Waddell became a sportswriter for the Evening Citizen and Scottish Daily Express.

From the mid-1960s Scottish football was dominated by the Celtic side managed by Jock Stein. In 1969 Waddell returned to Rangers as manager, following the sacking of Davie White. The Ibrox team did not win any league championships with Waddell as manager, but won the Scottish League Cup in 1971, ending a barren run of six years without a trophy. In 1972 Waddell led Rangers to their most famous victory when they won the European Cup Winners' Cup, beating Dynamo Moscow 3–2 in the final in Barcelona. Later in 1972 he handed over the management reins to his assistant, Jock Wallace.

Waddell also served Rangers as general manager and vice chairman. During Waddell's time as manager, Rangers had endured the 1971 Ibrox disaster, when 66 fans lost their lives on Stairway 13. Waddell was credited with the reconstruction of Ibrox Stadium in the late 1970s and early 1980s, making it one of the most modern grounds in Europe at that time.

Willie's parents Walter Young Waddell and Grace Clarkston Stark Orr

The Waddell ancestry becomes quite convoluted due to successive illegitimacies. Willie's father Walter Young Waddell was born illegitimately on 27 August 1900 at Hailstonegreen, Carnwath, Lanarkshire, to mother Marion Waddell, a farm servant. In 1901 Walter, just 7 months old, still resided in the village of Hailstonegreen with his mother Marion Waddell, 31, a domestic servant, great-grandmother Marion, 77, a widow, great-uncle Walter, 53, a coal miner, cousins Hugh, 24, and twins Walter and Hugh, 11, scholars. When Walter left school he went into the Lanarkshire coalfields as a miner. Grace Clarkston Stark Orr was born on 1 December 1899 at Bank Buildings, Forth, Lanarkshire, to father William Orr, a grocer and drapery merchant, and mother Annie Stark. After schooling Grace went into domestic service.

Walter Young Waddell, 20, a coal miner, of Hailstonegreen, married Grace Clarkston Stark Orr, 20, a domestic servant, residing in Forth, on Guy Fawke's Day, 5 November 1920. The wedding was conducted by Rev Walter P Brock, minister of Forth Parish Church; the best man was William Wilson and the best maid was Margaret Orr, Grace's sister. Son William Tweedie Orr Waddell was born on 7 March 1921 at Orr's Buildings, Forth.

Willie's paternal grandmother Marion Waddell

Willie's paternal grandfather has not been identified and it is possible Willie never knew much about him. His grandmother Marion Waddell was also born illegitimately, although in this case the father of repute owned up. Marion, recorded as Gray, was born on 22 December 1870 at Forth, Carnwath, to father John Gray, a coal miner, and mother Grace Waddell, a farm servant. The near six week delay in registering the birth was probably to give John Gray a chance to accept the paternity.

Later Marion reverted back to the surname of Waddell, suggesting John Gray did not become a hands-on father. Marion Waddell, a farm servant, gave birth illegitimately to son Walter Young Waddell on 27 August 1900 at Hailstonegreen, Carnwath. In 1901 Marion Waddell, 31, a domestic servant, still resided in Hailstonegreen, with son Walter, just 7 months old, her grandmother Marion, 77, a widow, her uncle Walter, 53, a coal miner, cousin Hugh, 24, and twin nephews Walter and Hugh, 11, scholars. Marion Waddell, a housekeeper, never married and she was still alive in 1920.

Willie's maternal grandparents William Orr and Annie Stark

Willie's maternal grandfather William Orr was born around 1860, possibly in Lanarkshire, to father Thomas Orr, a miner, and mother Margaret Tweedie. His grandmother Annie Stark was born around 1867 to father Joseph Stark, a merchant, and mother Marion Nimmo. William Orr, 29, a coal mine engine keeper, of Climpsy, Forth, married Annie Stark, 22, also of Forth, on 28 June 1889. The wedding was conducted by Rev Walter P Brock, minister of Forth Parish Church; the best man was Thomas Orr, William's brother, and the best maid was Grace Stark, Annie's sister. Reverend Brock married two generations of Willie Waddell's ancestors.

William and Annie had two known daughters in Forth; Grace (b. 1 December 1899) and Margaret. Daughter Grace Clarkston Stark Orr was born on 1 December 1899 at Bank Buildings, Forth. By that time William was prospering and had developed his business in Forth as a grocer and draper. William Orr, a grocer and draper, and his wife Annie Orr nee Stark were still alive in 1920.

Willie's paternal great-grandparents John Gray and Grace Waddell

Willie's paternal great-grandfather John Gray was born around 1850. His great-grandmother Grace Waddell was born on 21 January 1852, in Carluke, to father Hugh Waddell and mother Marion Dempster. Grace was baptized on 22 February 1852 in Kirkton United Presbyterian Church in Carluke. In 1870 Grace fell pregnant by John, a coal miner, and she gave birth to an illegitimate daughter Marion. Daughter Marion Gray or Waddell was born on 22 December 1870 at Forth, Carnwath. Although, John Gray accepted the paternity it appears that he and Grace never married. Grace Waddell was probably dead by 1901.

Willie's maternal great-grandparents Thomas Orr and Margaret Tweedie

Willie's maternal great-grandfather Thomas Orr and great-grandmother Margaret Tweedie were both born around

1830 possibly in Lanarkshire. Thomas and Margaret had two known sons; William (b. ~1860) and Thomas. Thomas Orr, a miner, and his wife Margaret Orr nee Tweedie were both still alive in 1889.

Willie's maternal great-grandparents Joseph Stark and Marion Nimmo

Willie's other maternal great-grandfather Joseph Stark and great-grandmother Marion Nimmo were both born around 1840 possibly in Lanarkshire. Joseph and Margaret had two known daughters; Annie (b. ~1867) and Grace. Joseph Stark, a merchant, and his wife Marion Stark nee Nimmo were both still alive in 1889.

Willie's paternal great-great-grandparents Hugh Waddell and Marion Dempster

Willie's paternal great-great-grandfather Hugh Waddell and his great-great-grandmother Marion Waddell were born around 1824 probably in Douglas, Lanarkshire. Hugh and Marion had two known children; Walter (b. ~1848, Lesmahagow) and Grace (b. 21 January 1852, Carluke). By the turn of the century Hugh Waddell was dead but Marion Waddell nee Dempster was still alive. In 1901, Marion Waddell, 77, a widow, resided in Hailstonegreen, Carnwath, with son Walter, 53, a coal miner, granddaughter Marion, 31, a domestic servant, great-grandson Walter, just 7 months old, grandsons Hugh, 24, recorded as an 'imbecile', and twins Walter and Hugh, 11, scholars.

Chapter 7

Eddie Turnbull

(Queens Park, Aberdeen, Washington Whips & Hibernian)

Honours at Aberdeen:

1 Scottish Cup

Honours at Hibernian:

1 Scottish League Cup

2 Drybrough Cups

The young Eddie Turnbull

Edward Hunter Turnbull was born on 12 April 1923 at 12 Bothy Row, Carronshore, Bothkennar, Stirlingshire, to father James Turnbull, a coal miner, and mother Agnes Easton Jenkins. Turnbull enlisted in the Royal Navy during WWII, serving aboard HMS Bulldog, HMS Alnwick Castle and HMS Plover. For his bravery in the dangerous Arctic convoys, Turnbull was posthumously awarded an Arctic Star campaign medal in November 2015. Edward Hunter Turnbull, 28, a professional footballer, living at 56 Webster Avenue, Falkirk married his wife Caroline in 1953.

During the late 1940s and 1950s Turnbull was one of the Famous Five, the noted Hibernian forward line, along with Gordon Smith, Bobby Johnstone, Lawrie Reilly and Willie Ormond. At that time with Hibs he won three Scottish league titles. In 1955 he was the first British player to score in a European club competition. Turnbull was selected nine times to play for Scotland and played in the 1958 World Cup.

Turnbull the manager

Turnbull started his managerial career at Queens Park in 1963. He was manager of Aberdeen between 1965 and 1971 winning the 1970 Scottish Cup and finishing second in the league in 1971. After that he returned to his beloved Hibernian, winning the 1972 Scottish League Cup final against Celtic. He also managed their famous 7–0 win over their Edinburgh derby rivals Hearts on 1 January 1973. Hibernian chairman Rod Petrie stated: *"No-one had made a greater contribution to the club than Turnbull."*

Eddie's parents James Turnbull and Agnes Easton Jenkins

Eddie's father James Turnbull or Hunter was born illegitimately on 1 December 1884 at Carronshore, Larbert, to mother Mary Hunter nee Turnbull. Mary, who was separated from her husband Robert Hunter, did not state who James's father of repute was and she raised him as James Turnbull. Eddie's mother Agnes Easton Jenkins was born just a few weeks earlier on 22 October 1884 at Kinnaird, Larbert, to father Alexander Jenkins, a coal miner, and mother Agnes Easton.

In 1891, James Turnbull, 6, a scholar, resided at Kinnaird, Larbert, with his widowed mother Mary T Hunter, 36, an outdoor worker, siblings Mary, 15, an outdoor worker, Edward, 14, a coal miner, William, 11, a scholar, Elizabeth, 9, a scholar, and George Turnbull, 4. When James left school he became a coal miner and was employed by the renowned Carron Company, famed for the carronade, a type of 19th century ship's cannon. James Turnbull, 22, a coal miner, married Agnes Jenkins, 22, a domestic servant, both of Kinnaird, Larbert, on 27 September 1907. The wedding was conducted by Rev Alexander K Watt, minister of Carronshore Parish Church; the best man was James Jenkins, Agnes's brother, and the best maid was Lily Cowan, Agnes's cousin.

James and Agnes had five known children at Carronshore, Larbert; Agnes Easton (b. ~1908), James (b. ~1910), Alexander Jenkins (b. 10 May 1918), Mary Doylie (b. 5 July 1920) and Edward Hunter (b. 12 April 1923). The gap in the births suggested that James may have served in the army during WWI, however, as a coal miner he was in protected employment and he still lived and worked at Carronshore during the war. James is listed in the Valuation Rolls for 1915-16 as follows:-

> *Valuation Rolls for the County of Stirling 1915-16, parish of Grangemouth: 15 Bothy Row, Carronshore, House: [Proprietor] Carron Company: [Tenant] James Turnbull, miner: [Yearly Rent] £3.4s.*

As the war raged on towards its bloody climax, son Alexander Jenkins Turnbull was born on 10 May 1918 at 15 Daisy Cottage, Carronshore, Bothkennar. Daughter Mary Doylie Turnbull was born on 5 July 1920 at 16 Bothy Row, Carronshore and son Edward Hunter Turnbull was born on 12 April 1923 at 12 Bothy Row, Carronshore. James

Turnbull, a retired coal miner, and wife Agnes Turnbull nee Jenkins were both alive and living at 56 Webster Avenue, Falkirk in 1953.

Eddie's paternal grandmother Mary Hunter née Turnbull

Eddie's paternal grandmother Mary Turnbull was born around 1855 in Larbert, Stirlingshire, to father William Turnbull, a carter, and mother Mary Doylie. Mary Turnbull, 20, a field worker, who signed with her 'x' mark, of Kinnaird, Larbert, married Robert Hunter, 24, a coal miner, of Carronhall, Larbert, on 23 October 1875. The wedding was conducted by Rev Duncan Ogilvie DD, of the United Presbyterian Church; the witnesses were Colin Nisbet and William Turnbull, Mary's father. Mary and Robert had four known children; Mary (b. ~1876, Larbert), Edward (b. ~1877, Larbert), William (b. ~1880, Larbert) and Elizabeth (b. ~1882, Bothkennar).

While Mary was carrying Elizabeth her husband Robert emigrated to America, possibly with the hope that Mary and the children would follow. That never transpired and two years later Mary gave birth to son James Turnbull, or Hunter, illegitimately on 1 December 1884 at Carronshore, Larbert. Mary stated that she was 'married to Robert Hunter, coal miner, who she says is not the father of the child and further that she had no personal communication with him for three years, during which time he has been in America'. Mary did not state who James's father of repute was. Two years later she gave birth illegitimately to another son George Turnbull, or Hunter, on 28 November 1886 at Kinnaird, Larbert. Mary Hunter again stated 'her husband Robert Hunter is in America, she has not seen him for five years'.

Life was tough for Mary and she had to toil in the fields to make ends meet and raise her six children alone. In 1891, Mary T Hunter, 36, a widow and outdoor worker, resided at Kinnaird, Larbert with children Mary, 15, an outdoor worker, Edward, 14, a coal miner, William, 11, a scholar, Elizabeth, 9, a scholar, James Turnbull, 6, a scholar, and George Turnbull, 4. Mary Hunter nee Turnbull was still alive in 1916 and living three doors away from son James at Carronshore in the Valuation Rolls, as follows:-

> *Valuation Rolls for the County of Stirling 1915-16, parish of Grangemouth: 18 Bothy Row, Carronshore, House: [Proprietor] Carron Company: [Tenant] Mary Turnbull, widow: [Yearly Rent] £4.3s.*

Eddie's maternal grandparents Alexander Jenkins and Agnes Wilson Easton

Eddie's maternal grandfather Alexander Jenkins was born on 18 October 1847 at Kinnaird, Larbert, to father Alexander Jenkins, a collier, and mother Elizabeth Jenkins. His grandmother Agnes Wilson Easton was born a few months later on 22 April 1848, also in Kinnaird, to father George Easton, a collier, and mother Janet Cowan. The births are recorded in the OPRs for Kinnaird as follows:-

> *OPR Births Larbert 485/2/271*
>
> *1847: Alexander Jenkin: Alexander Jenkin, collier, and Elizabeth Jenkin, Kinnaird, [born] October 18:*

[baptized] December 5: Witnesses John Oliver & Henry Turnbull
OPR Births Larbert 485/2/271
1848: Agnes Wilson Easton: George Easton, collier, and Janet Cowan, Kinnaird, [born] April 22: [baptized] May 2: Witnesses Henry Turnbull & Thomas Turnbull

Interestingly, the OPRs show Turnbull witnesses at both baptisms, which reveals a close knit bond between the Turnbull, Jenkins and Easton families in the village of Kinnaird. In 1851, Alexander, 3, resided at Black Row, Kinnaird with his father Alexander Jenkins, 40, mother Elizabeth, 39, siblings Elizabeth, 12, a scholar, Janet, 10, a scholar, John, 7, a scholar, and baby Robert, age one.

Alexander Jenkins, 20, a coal miner, married childhood sweetheart Agnes Easton, 20, both residing in Kinnaird, on 9 October 1868. The wedding was conducted by Rev William Park MD, minister of Airth Parish Church; the witnesses were Alexander and George Easton, Agnes's brothers. Daughter Agnes Easton Jenkins was born on 22 October 1884 at Kinnaird, Larbert. Alexander Jenkins, a retired coal miner, and his wife Agnes Wilson Jenkins nee Easton were both still alive and living in Kinnaird in 1907.

Eddie's paternal great-grandparents William Turnbull and Mary Doylie

Eddie's paternal great-grandfather William Turnbull and his great-grandmother Mary Doylie were born around 1820 probably in Stirlingshire. William Turnbull, a carter, married wife Mary Doylie and they had a known daughter Mary (b. ~1855) in Larbert, Stirlingshire. William Turnbull, a carter, and his wife Mary Turnbull nee Doylie were still alive in 1875.

Eddie's maternal great-grandparents Alexander Jenkins and Elizabeth Jenkins

Eddie's maternal great-grandfather Alexander Jenkins was born around 1811 and his great-grandmother Elizabeth Jenkins was born around 1812 both in Larbert, Stirlingshire. It is possible that Alexander and Elizabeth were related, given that the surname is of traditionally Welsh origin and not common in Scotland. Alexander Jenkins, a coal miner, married Elizabeth Jenkins around 1838. They had five known children in Kinnaird, Larbert; Elizabeth (b. ~1839), Janet (b. ~1841), John (b. ~1844), Alexander (b. 18 October 1847) and Robert (b. ~1850). In 1851, Alexander Jenkins, 40, a collier, resided in Kinnaird with wife Elizabeth, 39, children Elizabeth, 12, a scholar, Janet, 10, a scholar, John, 7, a scholar, Alexander, 3, and baby Robert, age one. Alexander Jenkins, a coal miner, and his wife Elizabeth Jenkins nee Jenkins were both dead by 1868.

Eddie's maternal great-grandparents George Easton and Janet Cowan

Eddie's other maternal great-grandfather George Easton and his great-grandmother Janet Cowan were both born around 1815 probably in Stirlingshire. George Easton, a coal miner, married Janet Cowan and they had three known children in Larbert; Agnes Wilson (b. 22 April 1848), George and Alexander. George Easton, a coal miner, and his wife Janet Easton nee Cowan were both alive and living in Kinnaird in 1868.

Chapter 8

Willie Ormond OBE
(St Johnstone, Scotland, Heart of Midlothian and Hibernian)

Honours at Scotland
3 Home International Championships

The young Willie Ormond

Named after his grandfather, William Esplin Ormond was born on 23 February 1926 at 32 Napier Place, Falkirk, Stirlingshire, to father Robert Doniston Ormond, an iron moulder, and mother Margaret McNaughton. Willie's senior career started out at Stenhousemuir in 1946, but he was soon signed by Edinburgh side Hibernian in November 1946. As a player, Ormond, along with Eddie Turnbull, was renowned as one of Hibernian's Famous Five forward line, winning three Scottish league championships in the late 1940s and early 1950s. He left Hibs in 1961 and finished his playing days at Falkirk in 1962.

He won six Scotland caps and played in Scotland's ill-fated venture to the 1954 World Cup finals. Ormond also represented the Scottish League. His brother Gibby played league football for Airdrie, Dundee United, Cowdenbeath, Alloa and also represented the Scottish League. Another brother Bert emigrated and represented New Zealand at international level in 1962.

Ormond the manager

After he retired from playing, Ormond became assistant trainer at Falkirk. In 1967, he was appointed manager of St Johnstone. He led the club to the 1969 Scottish League Cup final and third place in the 1970-71 Scottish League campaign. This meant Saints qualified for European competition for the first time in their history. Ormond's contribution to St Johnstone was recognised by the club naming the South Stand at McDiarmid Park in his honour. After a successful spell managing St Johnstone he was head-hunted by the SFA.

The SFA appointed Ormond in 1973 to replace Tommy Docherty after he signed for Manchester United. Ormond led Scotland to the 1974 World Cup finals in Munich. Scotland beat Zaire and famously drew with Brazil and Yugoslavia to return home as the only unbeaten team in the tournament. This remains the best ever performance by a Scotland team in World Cup finals. In May 1977 he resigned as Scotland manager and was appointed manager of Hearts – arch-rivals of his old team Hibs. Many Hearts fans at the time were unhappy given Ormond's background but he soon won them over. However, after he was sacked by Hearts in 1980, he moved to Hibernian as assistant to his old Famous Five colleague Eddie Turnbull. When Turnbull resigned that same year, Ormond took over at Hibs, but his health deteriorated and he was forced to retire soon after.

Willie's parents - Robert Doniston Ormond and Margaret McNaughton

Willie's father Robert Doniston Ormond was born on 21 February 1900 at 25 David's Loan, Falkirk, to father William Esplin Ormond, a bottler, and mother Mary Turner McMeechan. After schooling Robert went into a foundry as an iron moulder. Willie's mother Margaret McNaughton was born on 7 November 1902 at 8 Pitt Street, Leith, Midlothian, to father John McNaughton, a foreman galvaniser, and mother Janet McCallum. After schooling Margaret went into domestic service.

Robert Doniston Ormond, 25, an iron moulder, of 32 Napier Place, Falkirk, married Margaret McNaughton, 24, a domestic servant, of 143 Graham Road, Falkirk, on 5 June 1925 at the Manse, Russell Street, Falkirk. The wedding was conducted by Rev A Ross Taylor, minister of Grahamston Parish Church; the best man was Charles Ormond, Robert's brother, and the best maid was Elizabeth B Gottier. Robert and Margaret had three known sons in Falkirk; William Esplin (b. 23 February 1926), Gilbert, aka Gibby, and Robert, aka Bert. Son William Esplin Ormond was born on 23 February 1926 at 32 Napier Place, Falkirk.

Willie's paternal grandparents William Esplin Ormond and Mary Turner McMeechan

Willie's paternal grandfather, after whom he was named, William Esplin Ormond was born on 16 May 1870 at Beres Road, Forfar, to father Robert Ormond, a railway labourer, and mother Margaret Esplin. Willie's grandmother Mary

Turner McMeechan was born around 1876, probably in Stirlingshire, to father Charles McMeechan, a labourer, and mother Agnes Palmer.

William Esplin Ormond, 26, a bottler in Falkirk, married Mary Turner McMeechan, 22, a domestic servant in Linlithgowbridge, on 1 July 1898. The wedding was conducted by Rev William Burnett, Church of Scotland minister; the best man was David Ormond, William's brother, and the best maid was Agnes McMeechan, Mary's sister. William and Mary had two known sons in Falkirk; Robert Doniston (b. 21 February 1900) and Charles. Son Robert Doniston Ormond was born on 21 February 1900 at 25 David's Loan, Falkirk. In 1925, William Esplin Ormond, a bottler, and his wife Mary Turner Ormond nee McMeechan were both still alive and living at 32 Napier Place, Falkirk.

Willie's maternal grandparents John McNaughton and Janet McCallum

Willie's maternal grandfather John McNaughton was born illegitimately around 1866 possibly in Glasgow, Lanarkshire, to mother Jessie McNaughton, a cotton factory winder. John got a job as a galvaniser, a fairly new process in the Victorian industrial era, electrolysing metals such as aluminium to stop them oxidising. His grandmother Janet McCallum was born around 1867, again possibly in Glasgow, to father Gilbert McCallum, a general labourer, and mother Mary Johnstone. After schooling Janet got a job as a semolina packer. Imported foodstuffs like semolina and tapioca were becoming popular as puddings with the Victorian masses as trading throughout the Empire expanded and prices reduced through increased supply.

John McNaughton, 20, a galvaniser's labourer, of 14 Eglinton Street, Glasgow, married Janet McCallum, 19, a semolina packer, of 32 Cornwall Street, Kinning Park, Govan, on Hogmanay, 31 December 1885 at 24 Bruce Road, Pollokshields. The wedding was conducted by Rev James Wallace, minister of Plantation Parish Church; the best man was William McNaughton, John's brother, and the best maid was Matilda McLachlan. By the turn of the 20th century the family had moved from Glasgow to Leith, Midlothian.

Daughter Margaret McNaughton was born on 7 November 1902 at 8 Pitt Street, Leith. John McNaughton, a foundry warehouseman, was still alive in 1925, however, his wife Janet McNaughton nee McCallum was dead by then.

Willie's paternal great-grandparents Robert Ormond and Margaret Esplin

Willie's paternal great-grandfather Robert Ormond was born about 1843 probably in Forfar, Forfarshire, now Angus, to father Alexander Ormond, a labourer, and mother Susan Orchison. His great-grandmother Margaret Esplin was born about 1843, probably in Forfar, to father William Esplin, a cattle dealer, and mother Margaret Morrison.

Robert Ormond, 22, a farm servant, married Margaret Esplin, 22, a linen weaver, both of North Muir, Forfar on 3 November 1865. The wedding was conducted by Rev P Wright, minister of the United Presbyterian Church; the best man was John Esplin, Margaret's brother, and the best maid was Elizabeth Kerr. Robert and Margaret had two known sons in Forfar; William Esplin (b. 16 May 1870) and David. As the emerging railway network moved northwards through Scotland, Robert left farm labouring behind and worked as a railway labourer, almost certainly with the Great North of Scotland Railway Company.

Son William Esplin Ormond was born on 16 May 1870 at Beres Road, Forfar, to father Robert Ormond, a railway labourer, and mother Margaret Esplin. In 1898, Robert Ormond, a railway yardman, and his wife Margaret Ormond nee Esplin were both still alive.

Willie's paternal great-grandparents Charles McMeechan and Agnes Palmer

Willie's other paternal great-grandfather Charles McMeechan and his great-grandmother Agnes Palmer were born around 1845 probably in Stirlingshire. Charles McMeechan, a labourer, married wife Agnes Palmer and they had two known daughters; Mary Turner (b. ~1876) and Agnes. In 1898, Charles McMeechan and his wife Agnes McMeechan nee Palmer were both still alive.

Willie's maternal great-grandmother Jessie McNaughton

Willie's maternal great-grandmother Jessie McNaughton was born around 1840 and she had a son John McNaughton born illegitimately around 1866 possibly in Glasgow, Lanarkshire.

Jessie was working as a cotton factory winder at that time. Jessie also had another son William McNaughton. Jessie later married husband Alexander Roy, a lamplighter, although it is unlikely that Alexander was John's father of repute. Jessie Roy nee McNaughton was still alive in 1886.

Willie's maternal great-grandparents Gilbert McCallum and Mary Johnstone

Willie's other maternal great-grandparents Gilbert McCallum, a labourer, and Mary Johnstone were born around 1840 and they had a daughter Janet (b. ~1867) possibly in Glasgow. In 1886, Gilbert McCallum, a labourer, and his wife Mary McCallum nee Johnstone were both still alive.

Willie's paternal great-great-grandparents

Willie's paternal great-great-grandfather Alexander Ormond and great-great-grandmother Susan Orchison were born around 1815 possibly in Forfarshire. Alexander and Susan had a son Robert (b. ~1843) probably in Forfar. Alexander Ormond, a labourer, and his wife Susan Ormond nee Orchison were both still alive in 1865.

His other paternal great-great-grandfather William Esplin and great-great-grandmother Margaret Morrison were also born around 1815 possibly in Forfarshire. William and Margaret had a daughter Margaret (b. ~1843) and a son John probably in Forfar. William Esplin, a cattle dealer, and his wife Margaret Esplin nee Morrison were both still alive in 1865.

Chapter 9

Tommy Docherty
(Chelsea, Manchester United and Scotland
and many other teams)

Honours at Chelsea:
1 English League Cup
Honours at Manchester United:
1 English League 2 title
1 FA Cup

The young Tommy Docherty

Tommy Docherty was nicknamed 'the Doc' by press and fans alike. Named after his father, Thomas Henderson Docherty was born on 24 April 1928 at 96 Millerston Street, Camlachie, Glasgow, to father Thomas Henderson Docherty and mother Georgina Neillie Frame. Docherty was raised in Glasgow's infamous Gorbals district. The Gorbals of the 1930s Depression Era was synonymous with Glasgow's 'No Mean City' image of slums, deprivation and razor gangs. Docherty began his playing career with Shettleston Juniors.

The turning point came in 1946 when he was called up for National Service in the Highland Light Infantry. While completing his service, Docherty represented the British Army at football. On demobilisation, Docherty was offered a contract with Celtic in 1947. He later stated that Jimmy

Hogan, Celtic's coach, was his greatest influence. However, Docherty found first team places hard to come by at Celtic.

In November 1949, after spending just two years with Celtic, he joined Preston North End. With the Lilywhites he enjoyed the most successful period of his playing career, where he won the 1951 Second Division title and got to the 1954 FA Cup final. Docherty played for several clubs, including Arsenal and Chelsea, and represented Scotland 25 times between 1951 and 1959, including the 1958 World Cup finals. The Doc also played in the ill-fated game at Wembley in 1955 when England beat Scotland 7–2. Always a great wit and raconteur, Docherty later joked, alluding to the religious divide in the West of Scotland, that the cause of the defeat was the orange ball: *"The Rangers players wouldn't kick it and the Celtic players wouldn't touch it!"*

Docherty the manager

Docherty managed a total of 13 clubs between 1961 and 1988, as well as managing Scotland. In February 1961, he was offered the post of player-coach at Chelsea and was later appointed as manager. Docherty guided Chelsea to win the League Cup in April 1965 with a win over Leicester City. In 1971 he was appointed Scotland manager, however, in December 1972, when Frank O'Farrell was sacked by Manchester United, Docherty was poached and quit his job with Scotland to become manager at Old Trafford.

He managed to keep United in the First Division in 1972–73. However, the 1973–74 season saw United struggle and they were relegated to the Second Division. In the following season United returned to the top flight as Second Division champions. In 1975–76 they finished in third place in the First Division and also reached the 1976 FA Cup final. Docherty led United to the FA Cup final again in 1977, this time as underdogs against Liverpool, which United won 2–1. Shortly after, news broke that Docherty was having an extramarital affair with the wife of United's physiotherapist. He was sacked in a blaze of publicity in July 1977. After spells with Derby County, Queens Park Rangers, Aston Villa, Preston North End and Wolverhampton Wanderers amongst others the Doc retired from management at the end of the 1987–88 season.

Tommy's parents Thomas Henderson Docherty and Georgina Neillie Frame

Tommy's father Thomas Henderson Docherty was born on 30 May 1889 at 162 Boden Street, Bridgeton, Glasgow, to father Neil Docherty, a contractor's carter, and mother Jane Henderson. In 1891, Thomas, age one, still resided at 162 Boden Street, Bridgeton with his father Neil Docherty, 27, a carter with his own account, and his mother Jane, 29. Tommy's mother Georgina Neillie Frame was born around 1898 in Glasgow to father James Frame, a red lead painter, and mother Mary Neillie.

As the muddy slaughter of the Battle of Passchendaele entered its fifth day, Thomas Docherty, 27, a tube work labourer, married Georgina Neillie Frame, 18, both of 71 East Nelson Street, Camlachie, Glasgow, on 26 October 1917. The wedding was conducted by Rev David Watson DD, minister at St Clement's Parish Church; the best man was

John McGahan and the best maid was Maggie Newlands. Son Thomas Henderson Docherty was born on 24 April 1928 at 96 Millerston Street, Camlachie, Glasgow. Thomas and Georgina later moved their family to live in the Gorbals.

Tommy's paternal grandparents Neil Docherty and Jane Henderson

Tommy's paternal grandfather Neil Docherty was born on 22 June 1863 at 5 Hozier Street, Bridgeton, Glasgow, to father Daniel Docherty, a storekeeper, and mother Catherine McLaren. Tommy's grandmother Jane Henderson was born around 1861 in Bo'ness, Linlithgowshire, to father Thomas Henderson, a pottery kilnman, and mother Elizabeth Paul.

Neil Docherty, 24, a contractor's carter, of 215 Bernard Street, Bridgeton, Glasgow, married Jane Henderson, 24, a woollen power-loom weaver, of 42 Preston Street, Bridgeton, on 12 June 1885. The wedding was conducted by Rev Robert Campbell, minister of Calton United Presbyterian Church; the best man was Daniel McLaren, probably Neil's cousin, and the best maid was Agnes Watson. Son Thomas Henderson Docherty was born on 30 May 1889 at 162 Boden Street, Bridgeton, Glasgow.

In 1891, Neil Docherty, 27, a carter with his own account, still resided at 162 Boden Street, Bridgeton, Glasgow, with wife Jane, 29, and baby son Thomas, age one. Neil Docherty, and his wife Jane Docherty nee Henderson were both dead by 1917.

Tommy's maternal grandparents James Frame and Mary Neillie

Tommy's maternal grandfather James Frame and his grandmother Mary Neillie were born around 1870 possibly in Glasgow. After leaving school James was a red lead painter, working with a reddish paint with a high lead content, used for protecting metal pipes, tubes and girders from corrosion. It was discovered in the 20th century that it was highly toxic and many red leaders died of lead poisoning. James and Mary had a daughter Georgina Neillie (b. ~1898) in Glasgow. James Frame, a red leader, and mother Mary Frame nee Neillie were still alive in 1917, during WWI.

Tommy's paternal great-grandparents Daniel Docherty and Catherine McLaren

Tommy's paternal great-grandfather Daniel Docherty was born around 1839 in Campsie, Stirlingshire, to father Neil Docherty, a dyer, and mother Ann Paterson. His great-grandmother Catherine McLaren was also born around 1839 in Campbeltown, Mull of Kintyre, Argyllshire, to father Daniel McLaren, a seaman, and mother Catherine Fleming. Catherine could not read or write but she spoke both Gaelic and English.

Daniel Docherty, 18, a dyer, of 150 New Dalmarnock Road, Bridgeton, Glasgow, married Catherine McLaren, 18, of 43 Warnock Street, Glasgow, on Hogmanay, 31 December 1857. The wedding was conducted by Rev James G Stewart, minister of Calton United Presbyterian Church; the best man was John Docherty, Daniel's brother, and the best maid was Marion McLaren, Catherine's sister.

Daniel, by then a storekeeper, and Catherine had two known children in Glasgow; Neil (b. 22 June 1863) and Catherine, aka Cath (b. ~1868). Son Neil Docherty was born on 22 June 1863 at 5 Hozier Street, Bridgeton, Glasgow. In 1891, Daniel Docherty, 51, a cartage employer running his own business, resided at 215 Bernard Street, Bridgeton, Glasgow, with wife Catherine McL, 51, son-in-law John Stevenson, 23, an engineer, daughter Cath, 23, and baby granddaughter Cath Stevenson, 8 months old.

Tommy's paternal great-grandparents Thomas Henderson and Elizabeth Paul

Tommy's other paternal great-grandfather Thomas Henderson and great-grandmother Elizabeth Paul were possibly born around 1835 in Linlithgowshire, now West Lothian. Thomas and Elizabeth had a daughter Jane (b. ~1861) in Bo'ness, Linlithgowshire. Thomas Henderson, a pottery kilnman, was dead by 1885, however, his wife Elizabeth Henderson nee Paul was still alive.

Tommy's paternal great-great grandparents

Tommy's paternal great-great-grandfather Neil Docherty and great-great-grandmother Ann Paterson were born around 1810 possibly in Stirlingshire. Neil and Ann had two known sons in Campsie, Stirlingshire; Daniel (b. ~1839) and John. Neil Docherty, a dyer, and his wife Ann Docherty nee Paterson were both still alive in 1858.

His other paternal great-great-grandfather Daniel McLaren and great-great-grandmother Catherine Fleming were born about 1810 probably in Campbeltown, Mull of Kintyre, Argyllshire. Daniel and Catherine had two known daughters in Campbeltown; Catherine (b. ~1839) and Marion. Daniel McLaren, a seaman, and his wife Catherine McLaren nee Fleming were both still alive in 1858.

Chapter 10

Ally MacLeod
(Ayr United, Aberdeen, Scotland, Motherwell,
Airdrieonians and Queen of the South)

Honours at Ayr United:
2 Scottish League 2 titles
Honours at Aberdeen:
1 Scottish League Cup
Honours at Scotland:
1 Home International Champions

The young Ally MacLeod

Known as Ally, Alexander Reid MacLeod was born on 26 February 1931 at 273 Allison Street, Govanhill, Glasgow, to father William Hay MacLeod, a sewing machine manufacturer's clerk, and mother Jane Ann Smith. His family lived at 27 French Street, Clydebank, from the mid-30s, close to the Singer Sewing Machine factory, but the house was bombed during the Clydebank Blitz on 13 and 14 March 1941. The MacLeods evacuated back to Glasgow and later settled in Mount Florida, near to Hampden and Cathkin Parks. MacLeod, still a schoolboy, signed provisionally for, the now defunct, Third Lanark in 1947. He made his first-team debut against Stirling Albion at Cathkin Park on 6 November 1949. During his playing career MacLeod played for Third Lanark, St Mirren, Blackburn Rovers, Hibernian and Ayr United.

MacLeod the manager

MacLeod started his managerial career in 1966 at Ayr United. He took Ayr back to Scotland's top division, taking them to a Scottish Cup and a League Cup semi-final and also set their attendance record with 25,225 watching a 2–1 success over Rangers. In 1973, he was named Ayr's 'Citizen of the Year'. In 1975, after nine years at Ayr, he moved to Aberdeen where he guided them to a League Cup final success over Celtic.

MacLeod is best renowned for his time as the Scotland manager, including their appearance at the 1978 World Cup. In May 1977 the SFA appointed him manager of Scotland. He introduced himself to the squad with the blunt statement: *"My name is Ally MacLeod and I am a winner!"* In his first months in charge, Scotland beat England at Wembley and qualified for the 1978 World Cup from a group containing Czechoslovakia and Wales. Scotland's World Cup expectations gathered momentum with MacLeod orchestrating a wave of optimism, saying to the press his team would return with "at least a medal". Scottish comedian Andy Cameron recorded the hit song 'Ally's Tartan Army', reaching number six in the UK Singles Chart.

Around 25,000 Scots followed the national team to Argentina. However, the wave of optimism was soon crushed by, as MacLeod put it, a "rank bad" 3–1 defeat to Peru and a hapless 1–1 draw against Iran. To qualify Scotland needed to beat the Netherlands, eventual finalists, by three clear goals. MacLeod gave Graeme Souness his first game of the World Cup and was rewarded with a much-improved performance. When Archie Gemmill scored one of the greatest World Cup goals to make the score 3–1 to Scotland, qualification to the next phase looked possible. However, three minutes later the Dutch pulled a goal back. The game ended 3–2 and Scotland were eliminated on goal difference.

MacLeod's subsequent managerial career included spells at Motherwell, Airdrieonians and a return to Ayr from 1986 to 1989 when he again won the Second Division title. After a spell with Queen of the South he retired in 1992. MacLeod summed up his career by stating: *"I am a very good manager who just happened to have a few disastrous days, once upon a time, in Argentina."*

Ally's parents William Hay MacLeod and Jane Ann Smith

Ally's father William Hay MacLeod was born on 26 July 1891 at 310 Cathcart Road, Gorbals, Glasgow, to father Thomas Kerr MacLeod, a building contractor, and mother Janet Reid. After schooling William Hay MacLeod worked as a clerk with Singer's Sewing Machine manufacturers. Ally's mother Jane Ann Smith was born on 18 July 1894 at Archbank Cottage, Moffat, Dumfriesshire, to father Robert Smith, a farm foreman, and mother Christina Hope. After leaving Archbank Cottage where Robert managed the farm, Jane moved to Glasgow's south-side to work as a confectioner. William and Jane were both in their 30s when they met and fell in love.

William Hay MacLeod, 36, a clerk, of 273 Allison Street, Govanhill, Glasgow, married Jane Ann Smith, 33, a confectioner, of 15 Muirhouse Street, Pollokshields, Glasgow, on 14 July 1928 at 16 Well Road, Moffat. The wedding was conducted by Rev John L Farquhar, minister of Moffat Parish Church; the best man was Thomas MacLeod, William's brother, and the best maid was Teen Hope Smith, Jane's sister.

Son Alexander Reid MacLeod, aka Ally, was born on 26 February 1931 at 273 Allison Street, Govanhill, Glasgow. By the mid-1930s the family had moved to 27 French Street, Clydebank, to be closer to the offices of the Singer Sewing Machine factory, where William worked as a clerk. The Valuation Roll for Clydebank in 1935-36 is as follows:-

> *Valuation Roll for the Burgh of Clydebank – Year 1935-36*
> *7995: House 27 French Street: [Proprietor] Dalmuir and West of Scotland Estate Company: [Tenant] William H M'Leod: [Annual Rent] £21.18s.0d*

However, on the moonlit nights of 13 and 14 March 1941, Clydebank was heavily blitzed by the German Luftwaffe, targeting John Brown's shipyards and the Singer Sewing Machine factories, along with heavily populated districts. It was estimated that only about six houses in Clydebank did not suffer structural damage and French Street was severely bombed. Singer's timber yard was hit by incendiary bombs resulting in a huge fire, but munitions work and sewing machines were soon back in full production, although the evacuated workforce was scattered over Dunbartonshire,

Renfrewshire and Glasgow. The MacLeod family evacuated Clydebank and settled in Mount Florida, Cathcart, Glasgow, near to Hampden Park.

Ally's paternal grandparents Thomas Kerr MacLeod and Janet Reid

Ally's paternal grandfather Thomas Kerr MacLeod was born around 1852 in Govan, Glasgow, to father Duncan MacLeod, a cooper, and mother Annie Galbraith. In 1861, Thomas, 9, a scholar, resided at 83 Hospital Street, Gorbals, Glasgow, with father Duncan MacLeod, 57, a cooper, mother Annie G, 48, siblings Margaret, 24, a darner, Susan, 22, a darner, Jean, 7, a scholar, and niece Ann Horn, 5. After leaving school Thomas became a bricklayer, but he had ambitions to rise through the fast-expanding building trade.

Ally's grandmother Janet Reid was born around 1853, probably in Glasgow, to father Alexander Reid, a master calico block cutter, and mother Janet Smith. When she met husband Thomas she was working as a housekeeper. Thomas Kerr MacLeod, 22, a bricklayer journeyman, of 10 Govanhill Street, near Cathcart Road, Glasgow, married Janet Reid, 21, a housekeeper, of 292 Cathcart Road, Govanhill, Glasgow, on 12 June 1874. The wedding was conducted by Rev P Hately Waddell, minister of the Presbyterian Church; the best man was John Erskine and the best maid was Grace Reid, Janet's sister. Thomas and Janet had two known sons in the Gorbals; Thomas and William Hay (b. 26 July 1891).

Son William Hay MacLeod was born on 26 July 1891 at 310 Cathcart Road, Govanhill, Glasgow. Thomas had risen from being a 'brickie' to become a building contractor during a period of rapid house building in Glasgow's late Victorian era, when it became the Second City of the British Empire. He went on to become a master of works. Thomas Kerr MacLeod, a retired master of works, and wife Janet MacLeod nee Reid were both still alive in 1928.

Ally's maternal grandparents
Robert Smith and Christina Hope or Jackson

Ally's maternal grandfather Robert Smith was born around 1859 probably in Balmaclellan, Kirkcudbrightshire, to father John Smith, a ploughman, and mother Susan Petrie. His grandmother Christina Hope was born illegitimately on 23 August 1860 at Clanary, Kells, Kirkcudbrightshire, to mother Margaret Hope, a domestic servant. Christina's father of repute may have been surnamed Jackson as her mother originally called her Christina Jackson shortly after her birth. In 1861, Grace Jackson, 6 months old, resided at Clanary, Kells, with her mother Margaret Hope, 25, widowed grandfather David Hope, 65, a shepherd, Aunt Agnes, 33, a housekeeper, Uncle James, 20, a shepherd, and cousin Grace Gibson, 6, a scholar. The ancient farmlands at Clanary in Kells are mentioned in a charter of 1506 *'by George bishop of Candida Casa and of the Chapel Royal of Stirling....of the £5 lands of Clanarie, Maslach and Kerowra in the parish of Kirkcum'*. Christina later moved to Balmaclellan in Kirkcudbrightshire where she met Robert.

Robert Smith, 22, a ploughman, of Knockbarn, Balmaclellan, married Christina Hope, 21, of Drumwhirr

Toll Bar, Corsock Bridge, Balmaclellan, on 23 May 1882. The wedding was conducted by Rev George Sturrock, minister of Corsock Quoad Sacra Parish Church; the best man was Edward Smith, Robert's brother, and the best maid was Agnes Jane Coltart, Christina's half-sister. Robert and Christina had two known daughters in Moffat, Dumfriesshire; Christina Hope, aka Teen Hope, and Jane Ann (b. 18 July 1894). Daughter Jane Ann Smith was born on 18 July 1894 at Archbank Cottage, Moffat, Dumfriesshire.

At the time Archbank House in Moffat was owned by William Johnstone Esquire and Robert Smith, at Archbank Cottage, was the farm's overseer. Archbank House is now an A-listed building by British Listed Buildings. Robert Smith, a farm labourer, and his wife Christina Smith nee Hope were both still alive and living at 16 Well Road, Moffat in 1928.

Ally's paternal great-grandparents Duncan MacLeod and Annie Galbraith

Ally's paternal great-grandfather Duncan MacLeod was born around 1804 in Cromarty, Ross-shire, situated on the farthest west point of the Black Isle peninsula. Ally's great-grandmother Annie Galbraith was born around 1813 in the Barony parish of Glasgow. Duncan, a cooper or barrel-maker, migrated south to Glasgow around the 1830s, during the period of late 18th and early 19th centuries known as the Highland Clearances. Absentee landlords and clan chiefs were converting their lands, including Wester Ross, to more profitable sheep pastoralism and forcibly evicting tenants.

The Napier Commission of 1884, reporting on the lack of written evidence on tenancies, observed: *"It is difficult to deny that a Macdonald, a Macleod, a Mackenzie, a Mackay, or a Cameron, who gave a son to his landlord eighty years ago to fill up the ranks of a Highland regiment, did morally acquire a tenure in his holding more sacred than the stipulations of a written covenant."*

It appears Duncan MacLeod was married twice and had two known daughters by his first marriage in Glasgow; Margaret (b. ~1837) and Susan (b. ~1839). After the death of his first wife he married second wife Annie Galbraith around 1850 and they had two known children in Govan; Thomas Kerr (b. ~1852) and Jean (b. ~1854). In 1861, Duncan MacLeod, 57, a cooper, resided at 83 Hospital Street, Gorbals, Glasgow, with wife Annie G, 48, children Margaret, 24, a darner, Susan, 22, a darner, Thomas, 9, a scholar, Jean, 7, a scholar, and granddaughter Ann Horn, 5. The author's great-grandmother Georgina Caie Collie lived in Hospital Street in the 1920s, during the period when the infamous slums of the Gorbals gave Glasgow its violent reputation. Duncan MacLeod, a foreman cooper, was dead by 1874, however, his wife Annie MacLeod nee Galbraith was still alive in the Gorbals in 1874.

Ally's paternal great-grandparents Alexander Reid and Janet Smith

Ally's other paternal great-grandfather Alexander Reid and great-grandmother Janet Smith were born around 1825 in Lanarkshire. Alexander, a calico block cutter, and Janet had two known daughters in Glasgow; Janet (b. ~1853) and Grace. Alexander Reid, a master calico block cutter, and wife Janet Reid nee Smith were both still alive in Hutchesontown, Glasgow in 1874.

Ally's maternal great-grandparents John Smith and Susan Petrie

Ally's maternal great-grandfather John Smith and great-grandmother Susan Petrie were born around 1830 probably in Kirkcudbrightshire. John, a ploughman, and Susan had two known sons in Balmaclellan, Kirkcudbrightshire; Robert (b. ~1859) and Edward. John Smith, a ploughman, and wife Susan Smith nee Petrie were both still alive in Balmaclellan in 1882.

Ally's maternal great-grandmother Margaret Hope

Ally's maternal great-grandmother Margaret Hope was born on 24 September 1837 in Carsphairn, Kirkcudbrightshire, to father David Hope, a shepherd, and mother Grace Good. Margaret Hope, a domestic servant, gave birth illegitimately to daughter Christina Hope on 23 August 1860 at Clanary, Kells, in the Stewartry of Kirkcudbright. The father of repute may have been surnamed Jackson as Margaret called her daughter Christina Jackson shortly after birth.

In 1861, Margaret, 25, resided at Clanary, Kells, with her widowed father David Hope, 65, a shepherd, sister Agnes, 33, a housekeeper, brother James, 20, a shepherd, daughter

Grace Jackson, 6 months old, and a niece Grace Gibson, 6, a scholar. Around 1865 Margaret married husband John Coltart, a ploughman, and she had three other known daughters; Agnes Jane (b. 20 February 1867, Kells), Margaret (b. 1 March 1872, Corsock Bridge) and Elisabeth (b. 12 January 1874, Corsock Bridge). Margaret Coltart nee Hope was still alive in Drumwhirr Toll Bar, Balmaclellan in 1882.

Ally's maternal great-great-grandparents David Hope and Grace Good

Ally's maternal great-great-grandfather David Hope and great-great-grandmother Grace Good, aka Grizzel, a Scottish dialectical form of Graceful, were born around 1795 in Kells, Kirkcudbrightshire. David Hope, a shepherd, married Grace Good around 1820 and they had nine known children; in Carsphairn, an unnamed daughter (b. 21 September 1821), William (b. 15 June 1825), Agnes (b. 2 February 1828), Robert (b. 5 May 1830), John (b. 17 June 1832), Margaret (b. 24 September 1837); and, in Kells, James (b. 5 November 1839), Jean (b. 29 October 1841) and Eliza (b. 31 July 1843).

By 1861 Grace Hope nee Good was dead and David was a widower. In 1861, David Hope, 65, a widowed shepherd, resided at Clanary, Kells with children Agnes, 33, a housekeeper, Margaret, 25, James, 20, a shepherd, granddaughter Grace Gibson, 6, a scholar, and granddaughter Grace Jackson, 6 months old.

Chapter 11

Jock Wallace
(Berwick Rangers, Rangers, Leicester City and others)

Honours at Rangers:
3 Scottish League 1 titles
3 Scottish Cups
4 Scottish League Cups
Honours at Leicester City:
1 English League 2 title

The young Jock Wallace

John Martin Bokas Wallace was born on 6 September 1935 at his Donaldson grandparents' miner's cottage at 146 Forthview, Wallyford, East Lothian, to father John Martin Wallace, a professional footballer, and mother Catherine Sinclair Veitch Donaldson. Jock Wallace senior, was a goalkeeper for Raith Rovers, Blackpool and Derby County. Wallace junior, also became a goalkeeper, earning the unique distinction of being the only player ever to play in the English, Welsh and Scottish cups in the same season in 1966–67. He played in the FA Cup and Welsh Cup for Hereford United and in the Scottish Cup for Berwick Rangers.

Wallace's first senior club was his father's old club Blackpool, then he signed for Workington in 1952, combining football with work in the local pit. National Service with the King's Own Scottish Borderers allowed Wallace to sign for local club, Berwick Rangers. Following character-defining military service with the KOSB in Northern Ireland and the jungles of Malaya, Wallace's playing career extended to Airdrieonians, West Bromwich Albion, non-league Bedford Town and Hereford United.

Wallace the manager

Wallace's managerial career began in 1966 as player-manager of Berwick Rangers. In 1967, he was famously player-manager of lowly Berwick Rangers, which defeated Rangers in the Scottish Cup, providing one of the greatest cup upsets in Scottish football. That achievement propelled Wallace into a coaching job at Hearts in 1968. In 1970 Wallace arrived at Ibrox to coach Rangers under manager Willie Waddell. Using his tough army physical training techniques he gave Rangers players gruelling fitness sessions on the dunes at Gullane. The partnership with Waddell was one that helped Rangers win the 1972 European Cup Winners' Cup.

Later in 1972, Waddell moved upstairs to become general manager and Wallace was appointed manager. In the club's centenary year he won the Scottish Cup. In 1974–1975, it was Wallace who presided over the Rangers team that finally broke Celtic's 'nine-in-a-row' period of dominance and won the League championship for the first time in eleven years. In seasons 1975–1976 and 1977–1978, Wallace took Rangers to two Scottish trebles. Wallace's leadership of Rangers saw the club regain the ascendancy it had enjoyed throughout much of its history, but Wallace unexpectedly resigned in 1978.

Wallace moved to Leicester City and steered the club to Football League Second Division title glory in 1980. In January 1981, he made an unsuccessful attempt to sign three-time European Footballer of the Year, Johan Cruyff. He returned to Scotland in 1982, taking charge of Motherwell. In November 1983 he returned to manage a Rangers side that, under John Greig, had consistently under-performed. In spite of capturing two league cups, Wallace's second spell with Rangers was a frustrating one as the club failed to dent the dominance of the New Firm of Aberdeen and Dundee United under Alex Ferguson and Jim McLean. Wallace was sacked by Rangers in April 1986. He then had short spells with Spanish side Sevilla in 1986–87 and Colchester United in 1988–90. Jock Wallace is still fondly remembered by Rangers fans as one of their club's great managers.

Jock's parents John Martin Wallace and Catherine Sinclair Veitch Donaldson

Jock's father John Martin Wallace was born on 13 April 1911 at 12 Old Row, Deantown, Inveresk, to father John Wallace, a coal miner, and mother Nellie Bridges. In 1915 Winston Churchill, First Sea Lord of the Admiralty, planned to open up a second front in Turkey to ease pressure on the Western Front. On 22 August 1915, ANZAC forces were sent in to reinforce the last major assault at the infamous Battle of Hill 60 at Gallipoli, but ultimately the campaign failed and Churchill was heavily criticised. That same day, Jock's mother Catherine Sinclair Veitch Donaldson was born on 22 August 1915 at 32 Buchanan Street, Leith, to father John Donaldson, a coal miner, and mother Wilhelmina Anderson Veitch.

Like his son, Jock senior also had a stint at working in the Lothian coalfields, however, he too made the breakthrough into professional football as a goalkeeper. He began his career at Raith Rovers, before moving south of the border in March 1934, signing for Blackpool, playing there for 14 years and recording 243 league appearances for the Tangerines. Shortly after signing for Blackpool, John Martin Wallace, 23, a professional footballer, of 10 New Row, Deantown, Musselburgh, married Catherine Sinclair Veitch Donaldson, 18, of 146 Forthview, Wallyford, on 7 July 1934 by warrant of the Sheriff Substitute of the Lothians and Peebles, in the presence of Francis Naples and Annie Killen or Cochrane. Son John Martin Bokas Wallace was born on 6 September 1935 at 146 Forthview, Wallyford, East Lothian.

Wallace fell out with the Blackpool board over contractual terms and he joined Derby County for a nominal £500 fee in February 1948. He left Derby for Leith Athletic in August 1948, returning to Edinburgh where he had guested for Leith's rivals St Bernard's during WWII. John Martin Wallace, a retired professional footballer, died in 1978.

Jock's paternal grandparents John Wallace and Helen Bridges

Jock's paternal grandfather John Wallace was born about 1890, probably in Inveresk and Musselburgh, to father John Wallace, a coal miner, and mother Wilhelmina Cochrane. John followed his father into the Lothian coalfields. His grandmother Ellen Bridges, aka Nellie, was born around 1891 also in Musselburgh to father Archibald Bridges, a gardener, and mother Helen Nelson. After schooling Nellie worked as a golf ball maker. Musselburgh had been a centre of golf ball manufacturing going back to the days of the old 'featheries' produced by Gourlays since the early 19th century. When the new 'gutty golf ball' arrived John Gourlay immediately switched production and these were soon being produced on an industrial scale in Musselburgh.

John Wallace, 20, a coal miner, married Nellie Bridges, 19, a golf ball maker, both of 26 New Row, Deantown, Inveresk, on April Fools' Day, 1 April 1910 at the Roman Catholic Chapel, Musselburgh. The wedding was conducted by Fr Patrick McGettigan, RC clergyman; the best man was David Wallace, John's brother, and the best maid was Susan Wallace, John's sister. John and Nellie had four known children in Inveresk and Musselburgh; John Martin (b. 13 April 1911), Janet McAllister (b. 27 November 1914), Jamesina Bridges (b. 25 August 1918) and Peter (b. 23 October 1919).

Son John Martin Wallace was born on 13 April 1911 at 12 Old Row, Deantown, Inveresk. Daughter Janet McAllister Wallace was born on 27 November 1914, during WWI, at 28 Forthview, Wallyford, Inveresk. John Wallace enlisted in the 1st Battalion Scots Guards during WWI and he rose to the rank of Corporal. John probably arrived with the regiment in 1915 and the Scots Guards then saw action in some of the worst battles on Flanders Field, including Aubers Ridge and Loos in 1915, the dreadful Battle of the Somme in 1916, Passchendaele in 1917 and the Second Somme in 1918. When daughter Jamesina was born in 1918, John was still on active duty in France. Daughter Jamesina Bridges Wallace was born on 25 August 1918, during WWI, at 38 Old Row, Deantown, Inveresk.

That month the Scots Guards regiment was involved in the final assault on the Hindenburg Line and the Canal du Nord and in October 1918 they were on the final push at the Battle of Cambrai. After the Armistice on 11 November 1918 they were posted as part of the British Army on the Rhine and were in Cologne until 1919. Corporal 18436 John Wallace was demobbed in 1919 and returned home to Musselburgh and the Lothian coal mines. After WWI, son Peter Wallace was born on 23 October 1919 at 38 Old Row, Deantown, Inveresk. John Wallace, a coal miner, and his wife Ellen Wallace nee Bridges were both still alive in Musselburgh in 1934.

Jock's maternal grandparents John Donaldson and Wilhelmina Anderson Veitch

Jock's maternal grandfather John Donaldson was born around 1889 probably in Leith, Midlothian, to father Robert Gardner Donaldson, a coal miner, and mother Martha Jane Dalziel. His grandmother Wilhelmina Anderson Veitch was also born around 1889, probably in Leith, to father James Veitch, a cooper, and mother Catherine Sinclair. John had started out working in the coal mines, but when he met Wilhelmina, who was working in a warehouse, he had made the breakthrough as a professional footballer. It is unclear which team John played for, but it may have been for Edinburgh's long-lost third side St Bernard's FC, which played at the Royal Gymnasium in Leith.

John Donaldson, 24, a professional footballer, of 39 North Fort Street, Leith, married Wilhelmina Anderson Veitch, 24, a warehouse woman, of 7 Fort Place, Leith, on 3 June

1913. The wedding was conducted by Rev J A Fleming MA FRGS, minister of St Thomas Parish Church; the best man was Daniel Veitch, Wilhelmina's brother, and the best maid was Janet Dickson Cleghorn.

Daughter Catherine Sinclair Veitch Donaldson was born on 22 August 1915 at 32 Buchanan Street, Leith. At this point in WWI, John had returned to coal mining, with his footballing days behind him. This may concur with him playing for St Bernard's because the club was suspended during WWI, as their Gymnasium ground was requisitioned by the War Department. John Donaldson, a coal miner, was still alive in 1934, however, his wife Wilhelmina Anderson Donaldson nee Veitch was dead by then.

Jock's paternal great-grandparents John Wallace and Wilhelmina Cochrane

Jock's paternal great-grandfather John Wallace and great-grandmother Wilhelmina Cochrane were born around 1860 probably in East Lothian. John, a coal miner, and Wilhelmina had three known children probably in Inveresk and Musselburgh; John (b. ~1890), David and Susan. John Wallace, a coal miner, and wife Wilhelmina Wallace nee Cochrane were still alive and living in Deantown, Inveresk in 1910.

Jock's paternal great-grandparents Archibald Bridges and Helen Nelson

Jock's other paternal great-grandfather Archibald Bridges and great-grandmother Helen Nelson were born about

1860 probably in East Lothian. Archie, a gardener, and Helen had a known daughter Ellen aka Nellie (b. ~1891) in Musselburgh. Archibald Bridges, a gardener, and wife Helen Bridges nee Nelson were still alive and living in Deantown, Inveresk in 1910.

Jock's maternal great-grandparents Robert Gardner Donaldson and Martha Jane Dalziel

Jock's maternal great-grandfather Robert Gardner Donaldson and great-grandmother Martha Jane Dalziel were born around 1860 probably in Midlothian. Son John Donaldson was born around 1889 probably in Leith, Midlothian. Robert Gardner Donaldson, a coal miner, and wife Martha Jane Donaldson nee Dalziel were still alive and living in Leith in 1913.

Jock's maternal great-grandparents James Veitch and Catherine Sinclair

Jock's maternal great-grandfather James Veitch was born around 1846 in South Leith, Midlothian and great-grandmother Catherine Sinclair was born around 1845 probably in Midothian. James, a cooper or barrel-maker, and Catherine had three known children in Leith; Georgina Sinclair (b. ~1872), Wilhelmina Anderson (b. ~1889) and Daniel. James Veitch, a cooper, and his wife Catherine Veitch nee Sinclair were dead by 1913.

Chapter 12

Jim McLean
(Dundee United)

Honours at Dundee United:
1 Scottish Premier League title
2 Scottish League Cups

The young Jim McLean

McLean was the second of three sons of Tom and Annie and he grew up in the village of Ashgill. James Yuille McLean was born on 2 August 1937 at 6 Douglas Drive, Ashgill, Dalserf, Lanarkshire, to father Thomas McLean, a baker, and mother Annie Smith Yuille. His maternal grandfather William Yuille played professionally for Rangers before WWI. His father Tom had been a promising junior footballer before joining the Plymouth Brethren when he married Annie. Their three sons Willie, Jim and Tommy, who all went on to become professional footballers and managers, had a strict religious upbringing. After schooling, McLean served an apprenticeship as a joiner, a career he pursued part-time.

McLean's football career began with local juniors Larkhall Thistle, the third member of the family to play for Larkhall, after his father and brother Willie. In 1956, he started his senior career with Hamilton Academicals before joining Clyde in 1960. After leaving Clyde, McLean transferred to Dundee in 1965. McLean moved to his final club Kilmarnock, where he played alongside his brother Tommy. He retired from playing in 1970 and returned to Dundee as a coach in July 1970.

McLean the manager

After coaching Dundee for 18 months, the club's local rivals Dundee United offered McLean the position of manager in December 1971. He managed United between 1971 and 1993, becoming the longest-serving and most successful manager in the club's history, winning three major honours. He led the club to their only Scottish League title in 1982–83, following on from League Cup wins in 1979 and 1980. In Europe, McLean's Dundee United reached the European Cup semi-final in 1984 and the UEFA Cup final in 1987.

McLean's achievements saw him win the first ever SFWA Manager of the Year award in 1987. In addition to his Dundee United duties, he was part-time assistant manager to Jock Stein with Scotland for four years, including at the 1982 World Cup. McLean became a Dundee United director in 1984 and chairman from 1988 until 2000, resigning after an altercation with a sports reporter.

Jim's parents Thomas McLean and Annie Smith Yuille

Jim's father Thomas McLean was born on 7 January 1913 at 50 Raploch Street, Larkhall, to father William McLean, a coal miner, and mother Barbara Hamilton. When Tom left school he worked as a baker. He had also been a promising junior footballer with Larkhall Thistle, as recorded by his son Tommy, who wrote: *"My father's side were no strangers to the beautiful game either, with his brother William playing for Third Lanark. My dad was a force to be reckoned with in his own right in the juniors....most considered him to be the top McLean."*

Three months into WWI, the 'Battle of the Bees' was fought between British, Indian and German forces at Tanga, Tanzania on 4 November 1914. So named because a huge beehive was disturbed during the battle and both offensive British and defensive Germans were attacked by bees. That same day, Jim's mother Annie Smith Yuille was born on 4 November 1914 at Red Row, Dalserf, to father William Yuille, a coal miner, and mother Mary Marshall.

Thomas McLean, 21, a baker, of 44 Raploch Street, Larkhall, married Annie Smith Yuille, 19, a weaving factory hand, of 6 Douglas Drive, Ashgill, Dalserf, on 27 April 1934 in the Miner's Welfare Institute, Ashgill. The wedding was conducted by Pastor Robert Chapman of the Dalserf Christian Brethern; the best man was David Hamilton, Tom's cousin, and the best maid was Mary Gwynne Yuille, Annie's sister. Tom converted to the Christian Brethern and he and Annie brought their family up in the strict religious order. Tom and Annie had three sons in Larkhall; William, aka Willie (b. 2 April 1935), James Yuille, aka Jim (b. 2 August 1937) and Thomas, aka Tommy (b. 2 June 1947). Although the boys were raised in the strict Plymouth Brethern sect they all went on to become successful professional footballers and managers.

Jim's paternal grandparents William McLean and Barbara Hamilton

Jim's paternal grandfather William McLean was born on 18 June 1889 at 106 Meadowhill, Larkhall, to father Thomas McLean, a coal miner, and mother Mary Brannan. Initially, William worked down the Lanarkshire coalfields but later became a railway surfaceman with the Caledonian Railway Company. Jim's paternal grandmother Barbara Hamilton was born around 1894 in Glasgow to father David Hamilton, a coal miner, and mother Elizabeth Hamilton. Barbara, like many girls of the Victorian era, went into domestic service.

William McLean, 23, a coal miner, of 24 Marshall Street, Larkhall, married Barbara Hamilton, 18, a domestic servant, of 30 Young Street, Glasgow, on 28 June 1912 at 90½ Great Hamilton Street, Calton, Glasgow by warrant of the Sheriff Substitute of Lanarkshire in presence of John Pate, a vanman, and Agnes Cook or Pate. Barbara was pregnant by William, which might explain the civil ceremony, and son Thomas McLean was born on 7 January 1913 at 50 Raploch Street, Larkhall. William and Barbara also had another son Willie who played for Third Lanark, whilst son Tom had a spell with Larkhall Thistle. William McLean, a railway surfaceman, was dead by 1934, however, his wife Barbara McLean nee Hamilton was still alive.

Jim's maternal grandparents William Yuille and Mary Marshall

Jim's maternal grandfather William Yuille was born around 1889 possibly in Dalserf, Lanarkshire, to father James

Yuille, a coal miner, and mother Annie Smith. Between 1908 and 1911 William Yuille played professionally with Rangers making his league debut on 12 December 1908 against Hamilton Academicals. Grandson Tommy McLean, European Cup Winners' Cup medallist with Rangers in 1972, wrote: *"My mother's father, William Yuille, was a forward with Rangers and scored a few goals by all accounts."* Actually, William did not quite make the breakthrough at Rangers, playing only 16 first team games and scoring six times. William went back to coal mining and Tommy described him in the Scotsman as *'an auld bugger who was very strict'*.

Jim's grandmother Mary Marshall was born around 1891, also in Dalserf, to father William Marshall and mother Mary Gwynne. William Yuille, 22, a coal miner, of Red Row, Dalserf, married Mary Marshall, 20, a domestic servant, of Tinto View, Dalserf, on 10 March 1911. The wedding was conducted by Rev Alexander Barclay BD, minister of Dalserf Parish Church; the best man was Robert Yuille, William's brother, and the best maid was Elizabeth Marshall, Mary's sister.

William and Mary had two known daughters; Annie Smith (b. 4 November 1914) and Mary Gwynne. Three months after the outbreak of WWI, daughter Annie Smith Yuille was born on 4 November 1914 at Red Row, Dalserf. William Yuille, a motor vanman, was still alive in 1934, however, his wife Mary Yuille nee Marshall was dead by then.

Jim's paternal great-grandparents Thomas McLean and Mary Brannan

Jim's paternal great-grandfather Thomas McLean was born on 7 June 1864 in Cambusnethan, Lanarkshire, to father

William McLean, a coal miner, and mother Jane McCombs. Jim's great-grandmother Mary Brannan was born on 25 May 1860 in Shotts, Lanarkshire, to father James Brannan, a coal miner, and mother Catherine Higgins. William McLean, 19, a coal miner, married Mary Brannan, 19, a farm servant, both of Merryton Colliery Row, Hamilton, on 10 January 1884 at County Buildings, Hamilton by warrant of the Sheriff Substitute for Lanarkshire in presence of Alexander McCormick, a miner, and Isabella Davidson McCormick.

The likelihood is this was a mixed marriage, which might explain the civil ceremony. Son William McLean was born on 18 June 1889 at 106 Meadowhill, Larkhall. Thomas McLean, a coal miner, was still alive in 1912, however, his wife Mary McLean nee Brannan was dead by then.

Jim's paternal great-grandparents David Hamilton and Elizabeth Hamilton

Jim's other paternal great-grandfather David Hamilton and his great-grandmother Elizabeth, also surnamed Hamilton, were both born around 1865 possibly in Glasgow. David and Elizabeth had a daughter Barbara (b. ~1894) possibly in Glasgow. David Hamilton, a coal miner, and his wife Elizabeth Hamilton nee Hamilton were both alive and living in Calton, Glasgow in 1912.

Jim's maternal great-grandparents James Yuille and Annie Smith

Jim's maternal great-grandfather James Yuille and great-grandmother Annie Smith were born around 1860 probably in Lanarkshire. James and Annie had two known sons possibly in Dalserf; William (b. ~1889) and Robert. James Yuille, a coal miner, and wife Annie Yuille nee Smith were both alive in 1911.

Jim's maternal great-grandparents William Marshall and Mary Gwynne

Jim's other maternal great-grandfather William Marshall and great-grandmother Mary Gwynne were born around 1865 probably in Lanarkshire. William and Mary had two known daughters possibly in Dalserf; Mary (b. ~1891) and Elizabeth. William Marshall, a coal miner, and wife Mary Marshall nee Gwynne were both alive in 1911.

Jim's paternal great-great-grandparents

Jim's paternal great-great-grandfather William McLean and great-great-grandmother Jane McCombs were born around 1835 probably in Lanarkshire. William McLean, a coal miner, married wife Jane McCombs on 31 December 1861 in Cambusnethan Parish Church and they had seven known children; in Cambusnethan, Sarah (b. 7 November 1862), Thomas (b. 16 June 1864), James (b. 31 March 1866), Margaret Docherty (b. 25 April 1868), William (b. 21 March 1870, died in infancy); and, in Dalserf, Janet (b. 29 March 1872) and another William (b. 18 April 1874). William McLean, a coal miner, and wife Jane McLean nee McCombs were both still alive in 1884.

Jim's other paternal great-great-grandfather James Brannan and great-great-grandmother Catherine Higgins were born around 1835 possibly in Ireland. James and Catherine, who were Catholic, had two known daughters in Shotts; Bridget (b. 30 June 1857) and Mary (b. 25 May 1860). James Brannan, a coal miner, was dead by 1884, however, wife Catherine Brannan nee Higgins was still alive then.

Chapter 13

Craig Brown CBE
(Clyde, Preston North End, Motherwell,
Aberdeen and Scotland)

Honours at Clyde:
2 Scottish League 2 titles
Honours at Motherwell:
1 Lanarkshire Cup

The young Craig Brown

On 1 July 1940 Hitler's Nazi Stormtroopers completed the occupation of the Channel Islands. That same day James Craig Brown, aka Craig, was born on 1 July 1940 at 493 Corkerhill Road, Corkerhill, Glasgow, to father Hugh Craig Brown, a schoolteacher, and mother Margaret Fleming Caldow. Less than 16 years later the author was also born in Corkerhill railway village, about 200 yards away from Brown's birthplace. He was raised in Hamilton and educated at the former Hamilton Academy.

Brown played in Scottish schools competitions and youth and junior international level, before joining Rangers in 1958 from Coltness United. He was moved to Dundee on loan in January 1960, being the first signing of Dundee manager Bob Shankly, Bill Shankly's brother. Brown stayed at Dundee for four and a half injury-dogged years. He signed for Falkirk in 1965 but ended his playing career in 1967 after five knee operations.

Brown the manager

Brown quickly showed a keen interest in coaching and became assistant manager of Motherwell in 1974. He got his first managerial job as part-time manager of Clyde in 1977 winning the Second Division championship, whilst also working as a primary school headmaster and lecturer in primary education. He returned to football full-time in 1986 when SFA Secretary Ernie Walker appointed him assistant manager to the national team alongside manager Andy Roxburgh. Brown was also in charge of Scotland's youth teams. In 1989, he coached Scotland's under-16s to the final of the 1989 FIFA World Championship and three years later coached the under-21s to the semi-finals of the 1992 UEFA European Championship.

Brown was appointed as manager of Scotland in December 1993, having been caretaker for games against Italy and Malta. Brown took Scotland to the 1996 European Championships and 1998 World Cup, the last time Scotland qualified for any major championship. He resigned in October 2001 and was replaced by German Berti Vogts. Brown managed Scotland for 70 international matches, more than any other Scotland manager. He was awarded the CBE in 1999 for services to football. He has two honorary doctorates in B Ed (Hons) and BA.

Craig's parents Hugh Craig Brown and Margaret Fleming Caldow

Craig's father Hugh Craig Brown was born on 18 February 1911 at 125 Albert Road, Langside, Glasgow, to father James Brown, a certified teacher, and mother Martha Lamont Craig. Hugh also followed his father into the teaching profession. Craig's mother Margaret Fleming Caldow was born on 9 May 1913 at 82 Pollok Buildings, Corkerhill, Glasgow, to father Robert Fleming Caldow, a locomotive stoker, and mother Mary Gibson.

Hugh Craig Brown, 28, a schoolteacher, of 123 Queen Victoria Drive, Scotstounhill, Glasgow, married Margaret Fleming Caldow, 26, a bookseller's assistant, of 493 Corkerhill Road, Corkerhill, Glasgow, on 16 August 1939 at Sherbrooke Church. The wedding was conducted by Rev George Johnstone Jeffrey, minister of Sherbrooke Church; the best man was James Lamont Brown, Hugh's brother, and the best maid was Mary Gibson Caldow, Margaret's sister.

Just 16 days later on 1 September 1939, Adolf Hitler marched into Poland and two days later Britain declared war on the Nazi Third Reich. Son James Craig Brown was born on 1 July 1940 at his grandparents' home at 493 Corkerhill Road, Corkerhill, Glasgow. At the time Hugh and Margaret were living at 'Sherbrook', Goshen, Stenhousemuir. Hugh later moved the family to Hamilton where he continued to teach.

Craig's paternal grandparents James Brown and Martha Lamont Craig

Craig's paternal grandfather James Brown was born around 1879 in Glasgow to father Robert Stevenson Brown, an auctioneer, and mother Margaret Smith Brown. After his own schooling James Brown went on to become a school-teacher. His paternal grandmother Martha Lamont Craig was born around 1882 in Oban, Argyllshire, to father Hugh Craig, a farmer, and mother Martha Crawford Lamont. James Brown, 29, a teacher, of 15 Westmoreland Street, Govanhill, Glasgow, married Martha Lamont Craig, 26, of Ardoran, Oban, on Hogmanay, 31 December 1907 at the Western Hotel, Oban. The wedding was conducted by Rev James Reid, minister of Dunollie Road United Free Church, Oban; the best man was Alexander Millar and the best maid was Jeanie Craig, Martha's sister.

James and Martha had two known sons in Glasgow; Hugh Craig (b. 18 February 1911) and James Lamont. Son Hugh Craig Brown was born on 18 February 1911 at 125 Albert Road, Langside, Glasgow. James Brown, a school headmaster, and wife Martha Lamont Brown nee Craig were still alive and living in Scotstounhill in 1939.

Craig's maternal grandparents Robert Fleming Caldow and Mary Bethel Gibson

Craig's maternal grandfather Robert Fleming Caldow was born on 14 October 1881 in Riccarton, Kilmarnock, Ayrshire, to father Robert Caldow and mother Margaret Fleming. Robert, aka Bob, followed his father onto the locomotive footplate with the Glasgow & South Western Railway Company and by the late 19th century the family moved to the newly-built model railway village of Corkerhill, serving the new G&SWR locomotive depot. His grandmother Mary

Bethel Gibson was born around 1885, probably in Ayrshire, to father John Gibson, a locomotive driver, and mother Jessie Baird Gilmour. The Gibson family also moved to live and work in Corkerhill on the Paisley Canal line.

Robert Fleming Caldow, 25, a locomotive stoker, of 64 Pollok Buildings, Corkerhill, Glasgow, married Mary Gibson, 22, a dressmaker, of 122 Pollok Buildings, Corkerhill, on 25 January 1907 at the Railway Institute, Corkerhill. The wedding was conducted by Rev Robert Nicholson Thomson, minister of St Bernard's Church; the best man was William Caldow, Robert's brother, and the best maid was Bessie Gibson, Mary's sister.

The author fondly remembers the Railway Institute lying between the white stucco tenements of Corkerhill Place and the red-bricked tenements of Corkerhill Terrace. It was multi-functional and had a village store, a workers' library, a bathhouse and a 'steamie'. It was also used for religious ceremonies and Sunday School. Although, the tenements had inside toilets, families had to use the Institute to go for a weekly bath. The Pollok Buildings were built in 1897 by the G&SWR in the English crow-stepped gable style but by the 1950s when the village expanded the street was renamed Corkerhill Place. The author was born at 19 Corkerhill Place and father Archie McGee raised his large family there. In 1970 the village was demolished to make way for a new motorway.

Bob and Margaret had two known daughters at Corkerhill; Margaret Fleming (b. 9 May 1913) and Mary Gibson. Daughter Margaret Fleming Caldow was born on 9 May 1913 at 82 Pollok Buildings, Corkerhill, to father Robert Fleming Caldow, a locomotive stoker, and mother Mary

Gibson. Bob Caldow, alongside the author's great-great-uncle, Jimmy McGee, another Ayrshireman, were recorded as locomotive drivers at Corkerhill Depot in the 1920s in '*Legends of the Glasgow and South Western Railway*' by David L Smith. Robert Fleming Caldow, a locomotive shed arranger, and wife Mary Bethel Caldow nee Gibson were still alive and living in Corkerhill in 1939.

Craig's paternal great-grandparents Robert Stevenson Brown and Margaret Smith Brown

Craig's paternal great-grandfather Robert Stevenson Brown and his great-grandmother Margaret Smith, also surnamed Brown, were born around 1850 possibly in Glasgow. Robert went on to become an auctioneer in Glasgow. Robert and Margaret had a son James Brown born around 1879 in Glasgow. Robert Stevenson Brown, an auctioneer, was dead by 1908, however, his widow Margaret Smith Brown nee Brown was still alive then.

Craig's paternal great-grandparents Hugh Craig and Martha Crawford Lamont

Craig's other paternal great-grandfather Hugh Craig and great-grandmother Martha Crawford Lamont were born around 1850 in the parish of Kilmore and Kilbride, Argyllshire. Hugh Craig was a farmer at Ardoran, Oban, Argyllshire, now the site of a large marina and holiday chalet village on the shores of Loch Feochan. Hugh and Martha had two known daughters at Ardoran; Martha Lamont (b. ~1882) and Bessie. Daughter Martha Lamont Craig was born around 1882 at Ardoran, Oban. Hugh Craig, a farmer, was dead by 1908, however, wife Martha Crawford Craig nee Lamont was still living in Oban at that time.

Craig's maternal great-grandparents Robert Caldow and Margaret Fleming

Craig's maternal great-grandfather Robert Caldow and great-grandmother Margaret Fleming were born about 1850 in Ayrshire. Robert joined the G&SWR as a locomotive fireman probably at Riccarton near Kilmarnock. Robert and Margaret had two known sons in Riccarton; Robert Fleming (b. 14 October 1881) and William. Son Robert Fleming Caldow was born on 14 October 1881 in Riccarton, Kilmarnock. After 1897 the family moved up to live at Pollok Buildings where Robert became a locomotive driver at the newly-opened Corkerhill Depot, later rising to become a locomotive inspector. Robert Caldow, a locomotive inspector, and wife Margaret Caldow nee Fleming were both still alive and living at 64 Pollok Buildings, Corkerhill in 1907.

Craig's maternal great-grandparents John Gibson and Jessie Baird Gilmour

Craig's other maternal great-grandfather John Gibson and his great-grandmother Jessie Baird Gilmour were born around 1855 in Ayrshire. John and Jessie had two known daughters probably in Ayrshire; Mary Bethel (b. ~1885) and Bessie. John Gibson, another locomotive driver on the G&SWR,

also moved his family to live and work in Corkerhill. John Gibson, a railway engine driver, and wife Jessie Baird Gibson nee Gilmour were still alive and living at 122 Pollok Buildings, Corkerhill in 1907.

Chapter 14

Walter Smith OBE

(Rangers, Everton and Scotland)

Honours at Rangers:
10 Scottish League 1 titles
5 Scottish Cups
6 Scottish League Cups

The young Walter Smith

Named after his grandfather, Walter Ferguson Smith was born on 24 February 1948 at Lockhart Maternity Hospital, Lanark, to father John Smith, a crane driver, and mother Elizabeth Burns Rogerson. Smith grew up at 43 Gardenside Avenue, Carmyle, Glasgow, and as a boy he was a fan of Rangers. After leaving school he was employed by the South of Scotland Electricity Board before launching his football career in the 1960s with junior team Ashfield. Smith was signed by Dundee United in 1966 and made his first team debut against Kilmarnock on 20 March 1967. Smith married his wife Ethel in 1971. His future coaching mentor Jim McLean became manager in December 1971, and the following month Smith's future managerial assistant Archie Knox became a teammate. He remained a regular for United until 1974, often in central defence.

In September 1975, he was brought to Dumbarton by manager Alex Wright and former Rangers player Davie Wilson. Wilson had worked alongside Smith's father at the local steelworks near the village of Westburn, Cambuslang, and latterly had been a teammate at Dundee United. Jim McLean brought Smith back to Dundee United in February 1977, however, a serious pelvic injury effectively curtailed his playing career at the age of 29.

Smith the manager

Smith developed his coaching skills as assistant manager to Jim McLean, at a time when Dundee United were Scottish champions and European Cup semi-finalists. While working with McLean, a notoriously hard-bitten manager, Smith developed a reputation for being a strict disciplinarian. In 1978, he was appointed coach of the Scotland Under-18 team and helped them to win the European Youth Championship in 1982. He became coach of the Under-21 team and was Alex Ferguson's assistant manager during the 1986 Mexico World Cup. Ferguson later commented on Smith, stating: *"There are few people in the game with his experience, knowledge and technical ability."*

In April 1986, Graeme Souness was appointed player-manager of Rangers and Smith became his assistant. He helped Souness guide Rangers to Premier Division and League Cup glory in 1986–87, another League Cup in 1987-88, the Premier Division and League Cup in 1988–89, a second successive league title in 1989-90 and another League Cup in 1990–91.

When Souness left for Liverpool in April 1991, Smith was appointed interim manager, then permanently in May 1991 after the club clinched its fourth title in five seasons. Six more league titles in succession followed under Smith's tenure, including a domestic treble in 1992–93. He also won both the Scottish Cup and the League Cup three times each. Smith took Rangers to the brink of the final of the Champions League in season 1992–93. He announced in October 1997 that he was to retire after a period of domination in Scottish league football, however, he was lured to Everton in 1998 for a less than successful spell with the cash strapped Goodison Park club. After leaving Everton in 2002, Smith returned to football in March 2004 when he had a short spell as assistant manager to Alex Ferguson at Manchester United at the end of the 2003–04 season, when United won the FA Cup.

Smith was appointed manager of the Scottish national team on 2 December 2004, succeeding Berti Vogts. Despite a revival of fortunes under Smith, where Scotland's world ranking improved 70 places and Scotland recorded a famous victory against France in a Euro 2008 qualifier at Hampden, Smith failed to take them to any major championships. The SFA did not want to lose Smith but his return as Rangers manager was announced on 10 January 2007. In the 2007–08 UEFA Cup, Smith booked Rangers into their first European final for 36 years in Manchester, although they lost 0–2 to Zenit St Petersburg. On 25 May 2010, he signed a one-year deal to continue as Rangers manager, with Ally McCoist to take control thereafter. In his final season as manager, Smith led Rangers to another domestic double, winning the League Cup and their 54th league championship.

In February 2012 Rangers entered into administration. On 11 November 2012 Smith returned to Ibrox taking on a role with the new company as a non-executive director. Smith was appointed non-executive chairman of Rangers in May 2013 but he resigned from the board just three months later.

Walter's parents John Smith and Elizabeth Burns Rogerson

Walter's father John Smith was born on 3 April 1919 at 13 Hamilton Road, Cambuslang, to father Walter Ferguson Smith, a locomotive brakeman, and mother Anna McCabe. Walter's mother Elizabeth Burns Rogerson was born on 10 December 1921 at Carmyle Farm, Lanarkshire to father John Rogerson, a labourer, and mother Elizabeth Brown.

John Smith, 27, an engineer's fitter, of 2 Borgie Crescent, Cambuslang, married Elizabeth Burns Rogerson, 24, a printer's machinist, of 43 Gardenside Avenue, Carmyle, on 17 October 1946. The wedding was conducted by Rev J Lyle Rodger, minister of Carmyle Church; the best man was Lawrence Smith, John's brother, and the best maid was Margaret Brown, of 25 Napier Street, Bletchley. Intriguingly, Napier Street in Bletchley was only a mile and a half from the top secret Bletchley Park, where Alan Turing and his team famously cracked the code of the German Enigma machine. Could Margaret Brown, probably Elizabeth's cousin on the Brown side, have been part of the famed codebreaking team and still living in Bletchley in 1946 a year after the war ended?

John and Elizabeth had a known son Walter Ferguson (b. 24 February 1948). Son Walter Ferguson Smith was born on

24 February 1948 at Lockhart Maternity Hospital, Lanark. At the time the family were living at 43 Gardenside Avenue, Carmyle. John Smith was by then a crane driver and he was known to have worked at the local steelworks near Westburn, Cambuslang, almost certainly the Hallside Steelworks, which was owned by Colvilles Ltd. Walter later related that his teammate at Dundee United, Davie Wilson, also of Rangers, had worked beside his father John at the steelworks. John later got a storeman's job with the South of Scotland Electricity Board. John Smith, an SSEB storeman, and his wife Elizabeth Burns Smith nee Rogerson were both still alive in 1971.

Walter's paternal grandparents Walter Ferguson Smith and Anna McCabe

Walter's paternal grandfather, after whom he was named, Walter Ferguson Smith was born on 30 December 1896 at Chapelmains, Cambuslang, to father John Smith, a black-smith journeyman, and mother Margaret Eadie. After leaving school Walter became a steelwork rigger, again most likely at the Hallside Steelworks, which at that time was owned by the Steel Company of Scotland. Walter's grand-mother Anna McCabe, aka Annie, was born around 1897, possibly in Cambuslang, to father Lawrence McCabe, a coal miner, and mother Helen Gallacher. After schooling Anna became a dairymaid.

Less than three weeks before the Armistice was signed to end WWI, Walter and Anna were married. Walter Ferguson Smith, 21, a steelwork rigger, of 71 Main Street, Cambuslang, married Annie McCabe, 21, a dairymaid, of 208 Main Street, Cambuslang, on 25 October 1918 at the Church of Scotland Manse, Cambuslang. Walter, who later became a locomotive brakeman, and Anna had two known sons in Cambuslang; John (b. 3 April 1919) and Lawrence. Son John Smith was born on 3 April 1919 at 13 Hamilton Road, Cambuslang. Walter Ferguson Smith, a locomotive brakeman, and wife Anna Smith nee McCabe were both still alive in 1946.

Walter's maternal grandparents John Rogerson and Elizabeth Brown

Walter's maternal grandfather John Rogerson was born on 17 July 1893 at 15 Polmadie Street, Hutchesontown, Glasgow, to father William Rogerson, a railway yardman, and mother Jemima McGhie. When John left school he got a job as a steelworker, most likely at the Hallside works owned by the Steel Company of Scotland. The author's wife's own Irish ancestors had moved up to Hallside from Workington and lived in the Tarry Rows in the village at the end of the 19th century. Walter's grandmother Elizabeth Brown was born about 1892 possibly in Cambuslang to father Hugh Brown, a ploughman, and mother Elizabeth Burns.

John Rogerson, 27, a steelworker, residing in the Caledonian Buildings, Newton, Cambuslang, married Elizabeth Brown, 28, a bleachfield worker, of Carmyle Farm, Old Monkland, on 29 December 1920 at the farm. The wedding was conducted by the minister of Carmyle United Free Church; the best man was Andrew Rogerson, John's brother, and the best maid was Maggie Brown, Elizabeth's sister.

Daughter Elizabeth Burns Rogerson was born on 10 December 1921 at Carmyle Farm. John Rogerson, a power plant attendant, and his wife Elizabeth Rogerson nee Brown were still alive in 1946.

Walter's paternal great-grandparents John Smith and Margaret Eadie

Walter's paternal great-grandfather John Smith was actually born illegitimately as John Campbell on 29 April 1861 at Cross Street, Stewarton, Ayrshire, to mother Agnes Campbell, aka Ann, a bonnet knitter. Ann later named the father of repute as John Smith, a journeyman plumber, and thereafter raised her son as John Smith. It was common in the 19th century for a woman to name a child after the putative father in order to let the world know who impregnated her. Thus, but for that quirk of tradition, Walter Smith may have ended up being Walter Campbell. After leaving school John Smith ironically trained to be a blacksmith.

Walter's paternal great-grandmother Margaret Eadie, aka Maggie, was born around 1863 in Cambuslang to father John Eadie, a fruit seller, and mother Margaret Scoular. When Margaret left school she went to work as a farm servant. John Smith, 24, a journeyman blacksmith, of West Greenlaw, Cambuslang, married Maggie Eadie, 23, a farm servant, of 73 Main Street, Cambuslang, on 11 June 1886 at 15 Merry's Row, Blantyre. The wedding was conducted by Rev Thomas Pryde, minister of Stonefield Church, Blantyre; the best man was Hugh Spiers and the best maid was Mary Spiers.

John and Maggie had three known sons; John Robert (b. ~1884, East Kilbride), Robert (b. ~1889, Cambuslang) and Walter Ferguson (b. 30 December 1896, Cambuslang). In 1891, John Smith, 28, a blacksmith who spoke Gaelic and English, resided at 11 Colebrook Street, Cambuslang, with wife Maggie, 26, sons John Robert, 4, and Robert, 2. Son Walter Ferguson Smith was born on 30 December 1896 at Chapelmains, Cambuslang, to father John Smith, a blacksmith, and mother Margaret Eadie. John Smith, a journeyman blacksmith, was dead by 1918, although, his wife Margaret Smith nee Eadie was still alive and had lived through WWI.

Walter's paternal great-grandparents Lawrence McCabe and Helen Gallacher

Walter's other paternal great-grandfather Lawrence McCabe and his great-grandmother Helen Gallacher were born about 1850 possibly in Lanarkshire, although likely of Irish descent. Lawrence McCabe, a coal miner, married Helen Gallacher and they had a known daughter Annie (b. ~1879) possibly in Cambuslang. Lawrence McCabe, a coal miner, and his wife Helen McCabe nee Gallacher were both still alive in 1918.

Walter's maternal great-grandparents William Rogerson and Jemima McGhie

Walter's maternal great-grandfather William Rogerson was born about 1852 in Lochmaben, Dumfriesshire, to father James Rogerson, a master tailor, and mother Helen Dryden. In 1861, William, 9, a scholar, resided in a large 6-windowed home, at Braegate, Lochmaben, with his father James Rogerson, 30, a clothier, Helen, 30, a clothier's wife, siblings James, 7, a scholar, Rachel, 4, a scholar, and Jane, 2. When William left school he went into the fast-expanding railway industry as a railway brakeman, eventually based at the Caledonian Railway Company's Polmadie Depot in Glasgow. Walter's great-grandmother Jemima McGhie was born about 1860 in Johnstone parish, Dumfriesshire, to father Thomas McGhie, a mason journeyman, and mother Elizabeth Douglas.

William Rogerson, 25, a railway brakeman, married Jemima McGhie, 18, both of 40 Polmadie Street, Hutchesontown, Glasgow, on 4 January 1878 at their home. The wedding was conducted by Rev Andrew Alston, minister of Cathcart Road United Presbyterian Church; the best man was Thomas Russell and the best maid was Jane McGhie, Jemima's sister. William and Jemima had four known children in Glasgow; Elizabeth (b. ~1878), James (b. ~1881), John (b. 17 July 1893) and Andrew.

In 1881, William Rogerson, 29, a railway guard, resided at 46 Calder Street, Govanhill, Glasgow, with wife Jemima, 21, daughter Elizabeth, 3, and son James, 3 months old. Son John Rogerson was born on 17 July 1893 at 15 Polmadie Street, Hutchesontown, Glasgow. William Rogerson, a railway yardman, and his wife Jemima Rogerson nee McGhie were both still alive in 1921.

Walter's maternal great-grandparents Hugh Brown and Elizabeth Burns

Walter's other maternal great-grandfather Hugh Brown and his great-grandmother Elizabeth Burns were born about 1850 possibly in Lanarkshire. Hugh Brown, a ploughman, married wife Elizabeth Burns and they had a known daughter Elizabeth (b. ~1892) possibly in Cambuslang. Hugh Brown, a ploughman, and his wife Elizabeth Brown nee Burns were both still alive in 1921.

Walter's paternal great-great-grandparents John Smith and Agnes Campbell

Walter's paternal great-great-grandfather John Smith was born on 13 March 1820 in Stewarton, Ayrshire to father Andrew Smith and mother Margaret Wallace. The birth is recorded in the OPRs for Stewarton as follows:-

> *OPR Births Stewarton 616/3/381*
> *1820: March 19th: Smith: John son to Andrew Smith in Town and Margaret Wallace his spouse Born 13 curr[ent]*

Walter's paternal great-great-grandmother Agnes Campbell, aka Ann, was born around 1820 in the parish of Ardchattan, Argyllshire, lying to the north of Oban. By about 1850, Agnes had moved to the Renfrewshire weaving village of Pollokshaws, south of Glasgow, where she gave birth to an illegitimate daughter Agnes (b. ~1851). Agnes then moved on to live and work in Stewarton as a bonnet knitter. By 1861 John Smith was a widower and working as a slater. In 1861, John Smith, 39, a widowed slater, resided at Cross Street, Stewarton with his mother Margaret, 66, a widow, his sister Jean, 16, a bonnet knitter, and a daughter Ann C Smith, 10, a scholar. Just two doors away Agnes Campbell, 41, a sewer, also resided on Cross Street with her daughter Agnes, 10, a scholar.

Agnes Campbell, a bonnet knitter, was pregnant at the time with John Smith's illegitimate son born as John Campbell on 29 April 1861 at Cross Street, Stewarton. Agnes later declared that John Smith was the putative father and thereafter raised her son as John Smith. John Smith, a slater and plumber, was dead by 1886, however, Agnes, aka Ann Campbell, a farm servant, was still alive by then.

Walter's paternal great-great-grandparents John Eadie and Agnes Campbell

Walter's other paternal great-great-grandfather John Eadie and great-great-grandmother Margaret Scoular were born around 1825 possibly in Cambuslang. John, a fruit seller, and Margaret had a known daughter Margaret, aka Maggie (b. ~1853) in Cambuslang. John Eadie and his wife Margaret Eadie nee Scoular were both still alive in 1886.

Walter's maternal great-great-grandparents James Rogerson and Helen Dryden

Walter's maternal great-great-grandfather James Rogerson, a master tailor, and his great-great-grandmother Helen Dryden were both born around 1831 in Lochmaben, Dumfriesshire. James and Helen had four known children in Lochmaben;

William (b. ~1852), James (b. ~1854), Rachel (b. ~1857) and Jane (b. ~1859). In 1861, James Rogerson, 30, a clothier, resided at Braegate, Lochmaben, with wife Helen, 30, a clothier's wife, children William, 9, a scholar, James. 7, a scholar, Rachel, 4, a scholar, and Jane, 2. Also living in the large six-windowed home was Englishman George Burns, 16, a tailor's apprentice. Just two doors away in Braegate lived Jane Rogerson, 75, a ploughman's widow. Jane was born around 1786 in Lochmaben and is very likely to be Walter Smith's great-great-great-grandmother. James Rogerson, a master tailor, was dead by 1878, however, his wife Helen Rogerson nee Dryden was still alive at that time.

Walter's maternal great-great-grandparents Thomas McGhie and Elizabeth Douglas

Walter's other maternal great-great-grandfather Thomas McGhie, a mason journeyman, and his great-great-grandmother Elizabeth Douglas were born around 1825 in Dumfriesshire. Thomas and Elizabeth had two known daughters; Jemima (b. ~1860) and Jane in Johnstone parish, Dumfriesshire. Thomas McGhie, a mason journeyman, was dead by 1878, however, his wife Elizabeth McGhie nee Douglas was still alive at that time.

Walter's paternal great-great-great-grandparents Andrew Smith and Margaret Wallace

Walter's paternal great-great-great-grandfather Andrew Smith was born about 1781 and his great-great-great-grandmother

Margaret Wallace was born about 1795 both in Stewarton, Ayrshire. Andrew Smith, a farm servant, was married to wife Margaret Wallace on 23 November 1815 in Stewarton by Rev Mr Douglas. The marriage is recorded in the OPRs for Stewarton as follows:-

> *OPR Marriages Stewarton 616/1/355*
>
> *1815: November 10: Andrew Smith, farm servant and Margaret Wallace both in Stewarton: Proclamation Days 2: Allowances to the Poor 4s. 2d. Married November 23: Minister Mr Douglas, Stewarton*

Andrew and Margaret had eight known children in Stewarton; Janet (b. ~1816), John (b. 13 March 1820), Margaret (b. ~1823), James (b. ~1825), Jean (b. ~1827, possibly died in infancy), Mary (b. ~1837), Agnes (b. ~1838) and possibly another Jean (b. ~1844). Son John Smith was born on 13 March 1820 in Stewarton, Ayrshire, to father Andrew Smith and mother Margaret Wallace.

In 1841, Andrew Smith, 60, an agricultural labourer, resided in New Street, Stewarton with wife Margaret, 46, children Jeanet, 25, Margaret, 18, James, 16, Jean, 14, Mary, 4, and Agness, 3. Andrew Smith was dead by 1861 as his wife Margaret Smith nee Wallace was a widow by then. In 1861, Margaret Smith, 66, a widow, resided at Cross Street, Stewarton, with her widowed son John, 39, a slater, daughter Jean, 16, a bonnet knitter, and granddaughter Ann C, 10, a scholar.

Chapter 15

Graeme Souness

(Rangers, Liverpool and many other teams)

Honours at Rangers:

3 Scottish Premier League titles

4 Scottish League Cups

Honours at Liverpool:

1 FA Cup

The young Graeme Souness

Graeme James Souness was born on 6 May 1953 at Simpson Memorial Maternity Pavilion, Edinburgh, to father James Simpson Souness, a glazier, and mother Elizabeth Carrie Ferguson. Souness was raised at 44 Saughton Mains Avenue, Edinburgh and supported local side Hearts and also Rangers. In the 1960s Souness supported the young Alex Ferguson while he was at Ibrox, probably unaware that his great-grandfather was also named Alex Ferguson. As a teenager, Souness played for local boys' club North Merchiston.

Souness's career began as an apprentice at Tottenham Hotspur under Bill Nicholson when he signed as a 15-year-old in 1968. Souness made only one first team appearance for Spurs and Nicholson sold Souness to Middlesbrough in 1972, where his tenacious style began to garner acclaim there. Jack Charlton was appointed Middlesbrough manager in May 1973. One of Charlton's first signings was experienced ex-Celtic midfielder Bobby Murdoch, a fellow Scot, whom Souness later cited as an important influence in the development of his playing style.

Souness's playing career is best remembered for his seven seasons at Liverpool starting in January 1978, where he won five League Championships, three European Cups and four League Cups. He was part of Liverpool's Scottish triumvirate that included fellow Scots Kenny Dalglish and Alan Hansen. Souness had a two-year spell in Italy with Sampdoria, which ended in 1986 when he took up the position of player-manager at Rangers.

Souness the manager

Souness was appointed Rangers' first player-manager in April 1986, succeeding Jock Wallace. He embarked upon a bold strategy of reclaiming the football ascendancy Rangers had been desperately seeking in Scotland after years in the wilderness, due to the dominance of arch-rivals, Celtic, and the emergence of the New Firm of Aberdeen and Dundee United. The 'Souness Revolution' began with a slew of major signings from English clubs, including Terry Butcher, Chris Woods, Trevor Francis and Ray Wilkins. In his first season, 1986–87, Rangers won the Championship and the League Cup, defeating Celtic 2–1 in the final. They retained the League Cup in 1987–88, defeating Aberdeen on penalties. Two more Championships were to follow, this time in seasons 1988–89 and 1989–90, and a further two League Cup victories.

In 1991, Souness left Rangers to take over as manager of Liverpool but he had major heart surgery in April 1992. Souness attended the 1992 FA Cup Final against the advice of his doctors and watched his Liverpool side win 2–0 playing Sunderland. Souness went on to manage various clubs including Galatasaray, Southampton, Torino, Benfica, Blackburn Rovers, where he won an English League Cup in 2002, and Newcastle United. He retired from management and took up a career as a TV pundit with Sky Sports and Irish channel TV3.

Graeme's parents James Simpson Souness and Elizabeth Carrie Ferguson

Graeme's father James Simpson Souness was born on 3 February 1920 at 95 Albert Street, Leith, Midlothian, to father Thomas Souness, a dock labourer, and mother Elizabeth Jane Brack Simpson. After leaving school James trained as a glazier. Graeme's mother Elizabeth Carrie Ferguson was born on 8 September 1922 at 7 Albert Street, Leith, to father William Ferguson, a general labourer, and mother Margaret Brown. The records reveal that James and Elizabeth both grew up in Albert Street in Leith. After Elizabeth left school she got a job in a local rope-work factory.

At the outbreak of WWII, James, working as a glazier, enlisted in the King's Own Scottish Borderers and he was engaged in war service when he married Elizabeth on 4 February 1944, the same day the Soviet 42nd Army captured the city of Gdov from the Germans. James Simpson Souness, 24, a glazier and Private, KOSB, still of 95 Albert Street, Leith, married Elizabeth Carrie Ferguson, 21, a rope worker, of 58 Sleigh Drive, Edinburgh, on 4 February 1944 at 1 Ettrick Road, Edinburgh. The wedding was conducted by Rev J E Hamilton, minister of St John's East Parish Church, Leith; the best man was Henry M McColl and the best maid was Margaret Ferguson, Elizabeth's sister.

James would have been quickly mobilised as the various battalions of the KOSB were at the forefront of the assault on Europe following D-Day on 6 June 1944 and the next couple of years must have been fraught times for his wife Elizabeth. Fortunately, James survived WWII and returned home to Edinburgh and back to work as a glazier. Son Graeme James Souness was born on 6 May 1953 at Simpson Memorial Maternity Pavilion, Edinburgh and the family lived at 44 Saughton Mains Avenue, Edinburgh.

Graeme's paternal grandparents Thomas Souness and Elizabeth Jane Brack Simpson

Graeme's paternal grandfather Thomas Souness was born on 30 June 1893 at 27 Bowling Green Street, South Leith, to father Adam Souness, a bonded warehouseman, and mother Jemima Watt. After schooling Thomas became a lorryman, which in those days would still have been as a horse-drawn carter. Graeme's grandmother Elizabeth Jane Brack Simpson was born around 1893, possibly in Leith, to father James Simpson, another lorryman, and mother Elizabeth Jane Johnston Edgar. Elizabeth went to work in an aerated water factory, the demand for which was becoming fashionable with Victorians.

On 3 August 1914 Britain declared war on Germany and entered the Great War. Around three weeks later Thomas

Souness, 21, a lorryman, of 8 Beechwood Terrace, Leith, married Elizabeth Jane Brack Simpson, 19, of 168 Albert Street, Leith, on 28 August 1914 at Brunswick Road Halls, Edinburgh. The wedding was conducted by Rev Thomas Porteous, minister of St James Parish Church; the best man was John Ferguson and the best maid was Williamina Thomson McGinnes. Thomas and Elizabeth had two known sons in Leith; Adam (b. 10 March 1916) and James Simpson (b. 3 February 1920).

Thomas soon enlisted and by spring 1916 he was attached as Private R4363415 to the Royal Service Corps Reservists, suggesting he was still on his basic training. While Thomas, normally a carter, was a serving soldier, son Adam Souness was born on 10 March 1916 at 5 Ferrier Street, Leith. It appears likely that after training Thomas Souness was posted as a gunner in the Royal Field Artillery and may have been promoted to 2nd Lieutenant RFA as listed in the London Gazette in March 1918. After Thomas was demobbed in 1919, he returned to Leith and then took a job in the Port of Leith as a dock labourer. Son James Simpson Souness was born on 3 February 1920 at 95 Albert Street, Leith.

Thomas Souness, a lorryman, and his wife Elizabeth Jane Brack Souness nee Simpson were still alive in 1944 when his son James was serving in the King's Own Scottish Borderers during WWII.

Graeme's maternal grandparents William Ferguson and Margaret Brown

Graeme's maternal grandfather William Ferguson was born around 1895, possibly in Edinburgh, to father Alexander

Ferguson, a carter, and mother Catherine Mearns. William also went on to work as a carter. Graeme's grandmother Margaret Brown was born around 1896, possibly in Edinburgh, to father Adam Brown, a joiner, and mother Mary Keddie. Maggie went to work as a wine warehouse woman. William Ferguson, 20, a carter, married Maggie Brown, 19, a wine warehouse woman, both of 13 Spey Street, Edinburgh, on 8 December 1905 at Pilrig Manse. The wedding was conducted by Rev George Macaulay, minister of Pilrig United Free Church; the best man was Alex Brown, Maggie's brother, and the best maid was Grace Kilpatrick.

William and Maggie had two known daughters Elizabeth Carrie (b. 8 September 1922) and Margaret. Daughter Elizabeth Carrie Ferguson was born on 8 September 1922 at 7 Albert Street, Leith. William Ferguson, a dock labourer, and his wife Maggie Ferguson nee Brown were both still alive in 1944.

Graeme's paternal great-grandparents Adam Souness and Jemima Watt

It is recorded in the appendix Glossary of Surnames that Souness is a rare Scottish border name. Graeme's paternal great-grandfather Adam Souness (or Sounes) was born on 1 September 1868 at Old Cambus, East Mains, Cockburnspath, Berwickshire, to father Thomas Souness, a ploughman, and mother Marion Edmond. His great-grandmother Jemima Watt was born around 1870, possibly in Leith, to father James Watt, a carting contractor, and mother Elizabeth Stirling.

In 1891, Adam, 22, a lorryman, resided at 14 Springfield Street, Leith, with his widowed father Thomas Souness, 62, formerly a farm servant, his sister Annie, 25, a housekeeper, and his brother James, 17, a vanman. Adam Souness, 23, a lorryman, of 226 Leith Walk, Leith, married Jemima Watt, 22, of 1 Bath Street, Leith, at her home on 3 June 1892. The wedding was conducted by Rev James Park, minister of St John's Parish Church; the best man was James Souness, Adam's brother, and the best maid was Agnes Dudgeon. Son Thomas Souness was born on 30 June 1893 at 27 Bowling Green Street, South Leith. Adam Souness, a bonded warehouseman, and his wife Jemima Souness nee Watt were both still alive in 1914.

Graeme's paternal great-grandparents James Simpson and Elizabeth Jane Johnston Edgar

Graeme's other paternal great-grandfather James Simpson and great-grandmother Elizabeth Jane Johnston Edgar were born around 1865 possibly in Leith. James, a lorryman, and Elizabeth had a known daughter Elizabeth Jane Brack (b. ~1895) possibly in Leith. James Simpson, a lorryman, and his wife Elizabeth Jane Johnston Simpson nee Edgar were both still alive in 1914.

Graeme's maternal great-grandparents Alexander Ferguson and Catherine Mearns

Graeme's maternal great-grandfather Alexander Ferguson and great-grandmother Catherine Mearns were born around 1855 possibly in Edinburgh. Alexander, a carter, and Catherine had a known son William (b. ~1885) possibly in Edinburgh. Alexander Ferguson, a carter, and his wife Catherine Ferguson nee Mearns were both still alive in 1905.

Graeme's maternal great-grandparents Adam Brown and Mary Keddie

Graeme's other maternal great-grandfather Adam Brown and great-grandmother Mary Keddie were born around 1855 possibly in Leith. Adam, a joiner, and Mary had two known children; Margaret, aka Maggie (b. ~1886) and Alex. Adam Brown, a joiner, was dead by 1905, however, his wife Mary Brown nee Keddie was still alive.

Graeme's paternal great-great-grandparents Thomas Souness and Marion Edmond

Graeme's paternal great-great-grandfather Thomas Souness (or Sounes or Suness) was born around 1822 stated as in St Ninian's, Stirlingshire and his great-great-grandmother Marion Edmond, aka May, was born around 1825 possibly in the parish of Abbey St Bathans, Berwickshire, in the Lammermuir Hills. Thomas Souness, a ploughman in Dunbar, and May Edmond, in Abbey St Bathans, were married on 7 April 1849 by Rev Thomas Davidson in Abbey St Bathans Church as recorded in the OPRs as follows:-

> *OPR Marriages Abbey St Bathans 726/2/49*
>
> *1849: Suness: Thomas Suness, of the Parish of Dunbar, and May Edmond, of this Parish, were, after*

proclamation in the Church of this Parish, married on the 7th April 1849 by the Revd. Thos. Davidson, Minister of this Parish. Witnesses present.

Thomas and May had three known children; Annie (b. ~1866, Innerwick), Adam (b. 1 September 1868, Cockburnspath) and James (b. ~1874, Cockburnspath). Son Adam Souness was born on 1 September 1868 at Old Cambus, East Mains, Cockburnspath, Berwickshire, to father Thomas Souness, a ploughman, and mother Marion Edmond. Marion Souness nee Edmond was dead by 1891. In 1891, widower Thomas Souness, 62, formerly a farm servant, resided at 14 Springfield Street, Leith with children Annie, 25, a housekeeper, Adam, 22, a lorryman, and James, 17, a vanman. Thomas Souness, a labourer, was still alive the following year in 1892.

Graeme's paternal great-great-grandparents James Watt and Elizabeth Stirling

Graeme's other paternal great-great-grandfather James Watt and his great-great-grandmother Elizabeth Stirling were both born around 1840 possibly in Leith. James, a carting contractor, and Elizabeth had a known daughter Jemima (b. ~1870) possibly in Leith. James Watt, a contractor, and his wife Elizabeth Watt nee Stirling were both still alive in 1892.

Chapter 16

Gordon Strachan OBE
(Coventry City, Southampton, Celtic, Middlesbrough and Scotland)

Honours at Celtic:

3 Scottish Premier League titles
1 Scottish Cup
2 Scottish League Cups

The young Gordon Strachan

Gordon David Strachan was born on 9 February 1957 in the Eastern General Hospital, Leith to father James Gordon Strachan and mother Catherine Livingstone Carse. Gordon was raised in a suburban housing scheme at 24 West Pilton Circus, Muirhouse, Edinburgh. His father Jim worked as a tubular scaffolder and his mother Catherine worked in a whisky distillery. Strachan supported Hibernian as a boy. At age 15, he damaged his vision playing football on the school playground when a pen became lodged in his right eye, almost costing him his sight. Strachan was initially offered a contract by Hibernian manager Eddie Turnbull, but his father Jim rejected it.

Strachan played for Dundee, Aberdeen, Manchester United, Leeds United, Coventry City and Scotland. In international football he earned 50 caps, playing in two World Cup final tournaments; Spain 1982 and Mexico 1986. At the age of 40, Strachan retired from playing in 1997, setting a Premier League record for an outfield player.

Strachan the manager

His managerial career started in 1996 with spells at Coventry City and Southampton, but after resigning in February 2004 he took a 16 month break. Strachan returned to management on 1 June 2005, when he succeeded Martin O'Neill as manager of Celtic. After a less than impressive start at Parkhead, Strachan coached Celtic to victory in the League Cup and in April 2006 Celtic won the Scottish Premier League title. Another two consecutive league titles followed in 2006-07 and 2007-08. Under Strachan, Celtic also won the Scottish League Cup twice in 2006 and 2009 and a Scottish Cup in 2007.

Strachan signed for Middlesbrough on 26 October 2009, but after poor results, he left by mutual consent on 18 October 2010. He was appointed manager of the Scotland national team on 15 January 2013, succeeding Craig Levein. However, the national side's qualification to a major tournament since Craig Brown took Scotland to the 1998 World Cup, eluded Strachan. He narrowly missed taking the Scots to the 2014 World Cup and to Euro 2016. After failing to qualify for the 2018 World Cup, Strachan resigned from his position on 12 October 2017.

It is left to Strachan's former Aberdeen and Scotland teammate Alex McLeish to take over the reins of the Scotland national team and possibly write a new chapter of Scottish managerial greats.

Gordon's parents James Gordon Strachan and Catherine Livingstone Carse

Gordon's father James Gordon Strachan was born around 1936 in Canongate, Edinburgh, to father Alexander Strachan, a postman, and mother Bridget Rafferty. Gordon's mother Catherine Livingstone Carse was also born around 1936 in Edinburgh to father David Wright Carse, a railway capstanman, and mother Jane Duncan. James Gordon Strachan, 19, a sawmill labourer, of 50 Granton Crescent, Edinburgh, married Catherine Livingstone Carse, 20, of 24 West Pilton Circus, Muirhouse, Edinburgh on 10 March 1956 at Granton Congregational Church, Boswall Parkway, Edinburgh. The wedding was conducted by Rev B A Cox; the best man was J S Nichol and the best maid was Isobel Carse, Catherine's sister. Jim and Catherine moved to 24 West Pilton Circus, Muirhouse, Edinburgh and Jim worked as a tubular scaffolder. Son Gordon David Strachan was born on 9 February 1957 in the Eastern General Hospital, Leith.

Gordon's paternal grandparents Alexander Strachan and Bridget Rafferty

Gordon's paternal grandfather Alexander Strachan was actually born Alexander Lundie Lamb on 5 September 1902 at the Royal Maternity Hospital, Edinburgh to father George Lamb, a coal salesman, and mother Agnes Slimman. The birth was registered by mother Agnes Lamb, of 50 Bristo Street, Edinburgh. Alexander never knew his father George as he had died on 9 April 1902. Gordon's grandmother, Bridget Rafferty, was born around 1905, probably in Edinburgh, to father Michael Rafferty, a general labourer, and mother Mary Ann Lavin. By the time Alexander married wife Bridget in 1929, he was working as a postman for the General Post Office, and he was then called Alexander Strachan.

Alexander Strachan, 26, a postman, of 3 St John's Hill, Edinburgh, married Bridget Lafferty, 24, a laundress, of 80 Canongate, Edinburgh, on 10 May 1929 at 11 Royal Terrace, Edinburgh. The wedding was conducted by Rev Archibald Morrison, minister of Abbey Parish Church; the witnesses were Joseph and Catherine Donoghue. Son James Gordon Strachan was born in 1936 in Canongate, Edinburgh, to father Alexander Strachan, a postman, and mother Bridget Rafferty. Alexander Strachan, a postman, was dead by 1956, however, his wife Bridget Strachan nee Rafferty was still alive by then.

Gordon's maternal grandparents David Wright Carse and Jane Duncan

Gordon's maternal grandfather David Wright Carse and his grandmother Jane Duncan were born around 1910 probably in Edinburgh. David and Jane had two known daughters in Edinburgh; Catherine Livingstone (b. ~1936) and Isobel. David Wright Carse worked as a railway capstanman, almost certainly with the London & North Eastern Railway Company. David was responsible for shunting wagons around the LNER goods depot and in 1947 he was transferred to British Railways under the post-war Labour government's nationalisation scheme. David Wright Carse, a railway capstanman, and his wife Jane Carse nee Duncan were both still alive in Muirhouse, Edinburgh in 1956.

Gordon's paternal great-grandparents George Lamb and Agnes Slimman

Gordon's paternal great-grandfather George Lamb was born around 1879 in Edinburgh, to father Charles James Lamb, a coal carter, and mother Elizabeth Kerr. George became a brewer's cellarman and then later a coal carter like his father. Gordon's great-grandmother Agnes Slimman was born around 1882 in Edinburgh, to father Charles Slimman, a grocer, and mother Agnes Lundie. On 21 July 1896 George Lamb, only 17, had the sad duty of registering the death of his father Charles from heart disease at the Edinburgh Registry.

George Lamb, 22, a brewer's cellarman, of 105 Dundee Street, Edinburgh, married Agnes Slimman, 19, of 91 Dundee Street, Edinburgh, on 17 May 1901 at All Saints Church, Brougham Street, Edinburgh. The wedding was conducted by Fr Alex D Murdoch, Episcopal priest; the witnesses were J S Nichol, Colin Campbell and Mary Slimman, Agnes's sister. In early 1902 Agnes fell pregnant but just weeks later tragedy struck, when husband George had a massive heart attack, possibly genetically inherited from his father Charles, who also died young of heart disease.

George Lamb, only 23, a coal carter, of 59 Lauriston Street, Edinburgh, died on 9 April 1902 at the Edinburgh Royal

Infirmary of cardiac asystole, aortic stenosis and incompetence for three months as certified by Dr Ian S Stewart MB. The death was registered by June Tripp, George's aunt, of 16 Eglinton Street. Five months later, Alexander Lundie Lamb was born on 5 September 1902 at the Royal Maternity Hospital, Edinburgh, as registered by George's widow Agnes Lamb, of 50 Bristo Street, Edinburgh. Agnes, who probably remarried, later changed her son's name to Alexander Strachan. Agnes Lamb nee Slimman was still alive in 1929.

Gordon's paternal great-grandparents Michael Rafferty and Mary Ann Lavin

Gordon's other paternal great-grandfather Michael Rafferty and his great-grandmother Mary Ann Lavin were born around 1875 probably in Edinburgh, although almost certainly of Irish descent. Michael and Mary Ann had a known daughter Bridget (b. ~1905) probably in Edinburgh. Michael Rafferty, a general labourer, and his wife Mary Ann Rafferty nee Lavin were still alive in 1929.

Gordon's paternal great-great-grandparents Charles James Lamb and Elizabeth Kerr

Gordon's paternal great-great-grandfather Charles James Lamb was born on 1 July 1856 in Edinburgh, to father Thomas Lamb, aka George, a stone quarryman, and mother Margaret Brown. His great-grandmother Elizabeth Kerr was born around 1856, probably in Edinburgh. Charles and Elizabeth had three known children in St George's,

Edinburgh; George (b. ~1879), Mary Ann Bellinger (b. 18 May 1881) and Benjamin Bellinger McPherson (b. 17 July 1891). Charles Lamb, a coal carter, died at West Port, Edinburgh on 21 July 1896 of mitral heart disease, for two years, and pneumonia, for seven days, as certified by Dr Robert A Fleming MD. Charles's wife Elizabeth Lamb nee Kerr, 66, died in Edinburgh in 1920.

Gordon's paternal great-great-grandparents Charles Slimman and Agnes Lundie

Gordon's other paternal great-great-grandfather Charles Slimman and his great-great-grandmother Agnes Lundie were born around 1855. Charles and Agnes had two known daughters in Edinburgh; Agnes (b. ~1882) and Mary. Charles Slimman, a grocer, and mother Agnes Slimman nee Lundie were both still alive in Edinburgh in 1901.

Gordon's paternal great-great-great-grandparents Thomas Lamb and Margaret Brown

Gordon's paternal great-great-great-grandfather Thomas Lamb and his great-great-great-grandmother Margaret Brown were born around 1820. Thomas and Margaret had four known children in Edinburgh; Charles (b. 1 July 1856), George Fotheringham (b. 23 April 1858), Thomas Henry (b. 14 May 1860) and Margaret Isabella (b. 23 April 1862). Thomas recorded as George Lamb, a stone quarryman, and mother Margaret Lamb nee Brown were dead by 1896.

Conclusion

This book celebrates the accomplishments of a group of Scotsmen who achieved extraordinary success in football management. It may be a long time before we see their likes again.

The family histories of these managers underlines the humbleness of their ancestry. Borne of men and women who criss-crossed Scotland to scratch a meagre living as agricultural labourers, coal miners, shipyard workers and domestic servants throughout the Victorian era. Poverty-stricken people who fought against hunger, disease and the threat of the poorhouse.

Into the 20th century their family histories tell of the struggle to survive during two devastating world wars and the desperate poverty during the Great Depression of the inter-war years. In many ways the family histories of these men and women are no different to our own stories. Most of us can trace our ancestry back to humble beginnings throughout the agrarian and industrial revolutions. What defines this book is the culmination of these specific family histories in producing 16 remarkable managers who went on to achieve some of the greatest British footballing achievements seen to date.

In conclusion, this book honours the greatest Scottish managers of the modern era.

Player References

Sir Matt Busby: the definitive biography, Patrick Barclay, 2017

It's Much More Important Than That: Bill Shankly, Stephen F Kelly, 1997

Jock Stein: the definitive biography, Archie MacPherson, 2014

My Autobiography: Sir Alex Ferguson, 2013

Kenny Dalglish: My Autobiography, 1997

Rangers: the Waddell Years, Stephen Halliday, 1999

Eddie Turnbull: Having a Ball, Eddie Turnbull & Martin Hannan, 2006

The Doc: My Story – Hallowed be thy Game, Tommy Docherty, 2007

More than Argentina: Authorised Biography of Ally MacLeod, Ronnie McDevitt, 2004

Big Jock: the Real Jock Wallace, David Leggat, 2014

Jousting with Giants: the Jim McLean story, Jim McLean, 1987

Football in the Blood: My Autobiography, Tommy McLean, 2013

Craig Brown: the Autobiography, Craig Brown & Bernard Bale, 1998

Silver Smith: the Biography of Walter Smith, Neil Drysdale, 2007

Graeme Souness – Football, My Life, My Passion, Graeme Souness, 2018

Strachan: My Life in Football, Gordon Strachan, 2007

Genealogical References

National Records of Scotland, General Register House, Edinburgh

FamilySearch.org – Church of the Latter Day Saints

National Archives, Kew, London

Online and Other References

The Mitchell Library

Dumbarton Library and Family History centre

ScotlandsPlaces.gov.uk

The Daily Telegraph

The Daily Record

The Guardian

The Scotsman

The London Gazette

Wikipedia.co.uk

Surname Database

House of Names.com

Scottishmining.co.uk

Fitbastats.com

Scottish Golf History

Legends of the Glasgow and South Western Railway, David L Smith, 1980

History of Corkerhill and the Paisley Canal, John McGee

British Listed Buildings

Singersewinginfo.co.uk

Glossary of Players' Origin of Surnames

Chapter 1: Busby – a surname of mediaeval Scottish origin and a locational name from the lands of Busby in the parish of Carmunnock, Renfrewshire. Likely to be named from the Old Norse "buski", bushes and "byr", homestead; hence, "homestead by a thicket of bushes".

Chapter 2: Shankly – from the descendants of an ancient Scottish tribe called the Boernicians. Shankly is a name for a person with long legs or a peculiar manner of gait. The surname was first found in Midlothian, where the family held a seat from ancient times. They were designated as "Shank of that Ilk", a clan who possessed lands of that same name.

Chapter 3: Stein – in Scotland this is both a surname which derives either from a local dialectal form of the personal name Steven (from the Greek "Stephanos" meaning "laurel wreath") or from the Norse "sten"- a stone. In Jock Stein's case it is from Steven.

Chapter 4: Ferguson – a surname of Old Gaelic origin, found in Ireland and Scotland, and is a patronymic form of Fergus, from the Gaelic personal name "Fearghus", composed of the elements "fear", man, and "gus", vigour, force, with the patronymic ending "son". This Gaelic personal name was the name of an early Irish mythological figure, a valiant warrior, and was also the name of St. Columba's grandfather.

Chapter 5: Dalglish – this unusual surname, with the variants Dalgliesh, Dalglish, Dagleas, Dagless and Daglish, is of Scots origin and is locational from a place "above the sources of the Tinna Water in the parish of Ettrick, Selkirk". It was first recorded in the 14th century in the form Dalglas and derives from the Gaelic "dail", field and "glas", green.

Chapter 6: Waddell – a surname of early mediaeval Scottish origin and a locational name from Weddale, the old name of the parish of Stow in Midlothian. The second element of the place name is from the Old Norse "dalr", a valley.

Chapter 7: Turnbull – this surname, mainly found recorded in Northern England and Scotland, is of Anglo-Saxon origin, and is a nickname for a man believed strong enough to turn back a charging bull.

Chapter 8: Ormond – a surname, with variant spellings Ormonde and Orman, with two possible origins. It may be an anglicized form of the old Gaelic-Irish surname "O'Ruaidh", composed of the elements "Og" meaning male descendant and "Ruaidh", red, referring to someone with red hair or complexion. At first it was known as O'Rooe but was altered by folk etymology to resemble a region in east Munster known as Ormond.

Chapter 9: Docherty – this is an anglicized form of the Olde Gaelic name O'Dochartaigh, the Gaelic prefix "Og" indicates "male descendant", plus the personal name Dochartaigh, from "dochartach" meaning "hurtful" or "obstructive". The leading sept of the O'Doherty clan belonged to County Donegal where they became Lords of Inishowen in the 14th century.

Chapter 10: MacLeod – this long established and noble Scottish surname is a development of the ancient Scots-Gaelic Mac Leoid. This is composed of Mac, meaning son of, and a Norse personal name Ljot-ulf, meaning "ugly wolf".

Ljotr was a Viking chieftain and Lord of the Isles who it is said also held lands in the Isle of Man.

Chapter 11: Wallace – a famous Scottish surname, which is believed to be an old Brittonic surname derived from the Norman French word 'waleis' meaning foreigner, which the Normans applied to the Welsh, Celts and Britons. The Celtic tribes from Hadrian's Wall to the Clyde Valley, where Sir William Wallace was born, were known as the 'walensis'.

Chapter 12: McLean – this notable surname, with spellings of MacLean, Maclean, MacLaine, McLean, Mccleane, McLane, etc., is widely recorded in Scotland and Ireland. It is a developed form of the Old Gaelic name "Mac Gille Eoin", which translates as "the son of the devotee of St John", from "Mac", meaning son of, and "gille", literally a servant or follower, and the saint's name "Eoin or Ian", the classic Gaelic form of John.

Chapter 13: Brown – recorded in many spellings from Brown, Broune and De Bruyn, to Brauner, Bruni and Brunet, this ancient and prolific surname derives from a pre-7th century Germanic and Anglo-Saxon word "brun" or Olde Norse personal name "Bruni". Originally this name would have been a tribal nickname for a person with brown complexion or hair.

Chapter 14: Smith – recorded in the spellings of Smith, Smithe, and Smythe this is the most popular surname in the English speaking world. Of pre-7th century Anglo-Saxon origin, it derives from the word "smitan" meaning "to smite" and as such is believed to have described not a blacksmith, but a soldier, one who smote. As he also wore armour, which he would have been required to repair, it may have led to the secondary meaning, i.e., that of a blacksmith.

Chapter 15: Souness – spelt as Suinhouse, Sounhouse, Sownes, Sounness, and Souness, this is a famous, but rare, Scottish surname. It is locational and probably originates from a place in ancient times called "Sun-hlaw" and now Sunilaw, in the Scottish Borders, near to the town of Coldstream. The name means the south hill, or possibly the sunny hill.

Chapter 16: Strachan – this name is of Scottish locational origin, from the lands of Strachan (pronounced "Strawan") in Kincardineshire. The name derives from the Gaelic "strath" meaning a valley, plus "eachain", the plural of "each" a horse, i.e., "the valley of the horses".

Glossary of Key Names

Chapter 1: Sir Matt Busby

Aston, John
Bayaert, Fr Arthur
Best, George
Brown, Elizabeth
Brown, Elizabeth sr.
Brown, Maria
Brown, Thomas
Burns, Catherine
Busby Matthew
Busby, Alexander
Busby, Alexander Matthew sr.
Busby, Alexander sr.
Busby, Bedelia
Busby, George
Busby, George sr.
Busby, James
Busby, Jane
Busby, Janet
Busby, Margaret
Busby, Matthew
Busby, Sir Alexander Matthew
Busby, Thomas
Busby, William
Carrol, Robert
Cassin, Fr Mortimer
Charlton, Bobby
Connelly, Agnes
Connelly, Bernard
Connelly, Margaret
Crerand, Paddy
Crine, Bridget
Crine, Michael
Crine, Peter
Crine, Thomas
Cronin, Fr Francis
Cumming, Patrick
Dale, Robin
Dewar, Alexander
Edwards, Duncan
Eusébio
Ferguson, Sir Alex
Gibson, James W
Greer, Bedelia
Greer, Ellen
Greer, Helen
Greer, James
Greer, James jr.
Greer, James sr.
Greer, Margaret
Greer, Mary
Greer, Thomas
Greer, William
Greer, William
Gregg, Harry
Kay, George
Kennedy, Margaret
Law, Denis
Mathie, Harry

Mathie, William
McGrogan, Margaret
McNeill, Billy
McPake, Catherine
McPake, Hugh sr.
McPake, Thomas
Mundie, Bernard
O'Hara, Bridget
Rocca, Louis
Taylor, Tommy
Walmsley, Jane
McConnell, Billy
McKennie, Mary
McPake, Bernard
McPake, Hugh
McPake, Maggie
McStay, Rose
Mundie, Mary
Paisley, Bob
Stein, Jock
Wagner, Rev W C

Chapter 2: Bill Shankly

Anderson, Rev George
Blyth, David
Blyth, Hannah
Blyth, Jimmy
Blyth, John sr.
Blyth, Robert
Busby, Sir Matt
Fleming, Janet
Gray, Barbara
Lyon, Grace
McLellan, Marion
Paisley, Bob
Shankly, Alexander
Shankly, Alexander sr.
Shankly, Bill
Shankly, Catherine
Shankly, Isobel
Shankly, Janet
Shankly, John
Shankly, Marion
Shankly, William
Smith, Rev William
Stein, Jock
Wight, John Brown
Blyth, Barbara Gray
Blyth, George
Blyth, James
Blyth, John
Blyth, Marion
Blyth, William J
Dunlop, Jane
Fleming, Robert
Harvie, William
McGarvy, Sophie
Neil, Sarah
Roberts, John
Shankly, Alexander jr.
Shankly, Andrew
Shankly, Bob
Shankly, Elizabeth
Shankly, James
Shankly, Jessie
Shankly, John sr.
Shankly, Sarah
Smith, John
Stark, Rev Thomas
Wight, Janet Brown

Chapter 3: Jock Stein

Aitken, Mary
Armstrong, Georgina
Armstrong, James
Armstrong, Jane McKay
Armstrong, John
Cameron, Rev P
Chalmers, Stevie
Cooper, Davie
Craig, Jim
Cross, Rev Alexander
Dempsey, Margaret
Ferguson, Sir Alex
Gemmell, Tommy
Hynds, Eliza
Johnston, Christina
Johnston, Elizabeth
Johnston, Margaret
Johnston, Robert
Johnston, William
Johnstone, Jimmy
Kelly, Sir Robert
Kilgour, Robert
MacGregor, Rob Roy
Mazzola, Alessandro
McGrory, Jimmy
McKay, Jane
Murdoch, Bobby
Powell, Jane
Raeside, John
Robertson, Mary
Russell, Janet
Scobbie, George
Scott, Rev Alexander T
Scouller, Georgina McKay
Scouller, John
Scouller, John sr.
Shankly, Bill
Sneddon, Marion
Sneddon, Robert
Somerville, Rev Thomas
Stein, Adam
Stein, George
Stein, Georgina Scouller
Stein, James
Stein, Jessie Scott Armstrong
Stein, John
Stein, John sr.
Stein, Margaret
Stein, Margaret Dempsey Johnstone
Stein, Margaret Johnstone
Stein, Mary
Stein, Robert
Steven, Adam
Steven, Adam sr.
Steven, Agnes
Steven, George
Steven, John
Steven, Marion
Steven, Mary
Steven, Robert

Steven, William
Thomson, William
Wilson, Robert

Chapter 4: Sir Alex Ferguson

Basler, Mario
Beaton, Alexander
Beaton, Janet Montgomery
Beckham, David
Blomqvist, Jesper
Cameron, David
Daly, Fr William
Fairley, Isabella
Ferguson, Alexander Beaton
Ferguson, Catherine
Ferguson, George
Ferguson, John
Ferguson, John sr.
Ferguson, Martin
Ferguson, Mary
Ferguson, Patrick
Ferguson, Robert
Ferguson, Robert sr.
Ferguson, Sir Alexander Chapman
Giggs, Ryan
Hardie, Alexander
Hardie, Archibald
Hardie, Elizabeth
Hardie, Mary Agnes
Hardie, Robert
Henderson, John
Hendry, Agnes
Holding, Catherine
Keane, Roy
Knox, Archie
Leighton, Jim
Macpherson, Rev A H
Mansell, Annie
Mansell, Susan
Mansell, Thomas James
McBride, Joe
McClaren, Steve
McFarlane, Mary
McGregor, Mary
McLeish, Alex
McNeill, Billy
Miller, Willie
Mulholland, Catherine
Mulholland, John
Notman, Rev Thomas
Platini, Michel
Prentice, John
Scholes, Paul
Scullion, Anne
Scullion, Elizabeth
Sheringham, Teddy
Shields, Winifred
Sibbald, Dr John
Solskjær, Ole Gunnar
Stein, Jock
Strachan, Gordon
Wilson, Dr James
Wilson, Fr R A

Chapter 5: Sir Kenny Dalglish

Borland, Elizabeth
Borland, Elizabeth sr
Borland, Mary Ann
Borland, William
Borland, William sr
Campbell, Rev John
Dalglish, Alexander
Dalglish, Catherine
Dalglish, David
Dalglish, David sr
Dalglish, James
Dalglish, Kenneth Matheson
Dalglish, Sir Kenneth Mathieson
Dalglish, William
Dalglish, William Borland
Davidson, Vic
Doyle, Mary Ann
Fallon, Sean
Gemmell, William
Gibb, Marion
Gray, Margaret
Hodgson, Roy
Laughlan, Elizabeth
MacDonald, Robert, PF Dep.
Macpherson, Rev Duncan
Malcolm, John
Malcolm, Matilda
Matheson, Catherine
Matheson, Helen
Matheson, Kenneth
McIntyre, Janet
McKay, Mary
Munro, Alexander
Munro, Catherine Rice
Munro, Donald
Munro, John Ewing
Munro, Marion Gibb
Paisley, Bob
Paterson, Helen Mathieson Dalglish
Paterson, William
Patrick, Rev Thomas A
Paxman, Jeremy
Ray, Joseph
Rice, Catherine
Rice, Margaret
Rice, William
Rice, William Andrew
Richardson, Mary
Smith, Rev William Chalmers
Stein, Jock
Tippon, Martha
Whiteford, Dr J
Yuille, Rev George Simpson

Chapter 6: Willie Waddell

Brock, Rev Walter P
Nimmo, Marion
Orr, Grace Clarkston Stark
Orr, Thomas sr.
Stark, Annie
Stark, Joseph
Tweedie, Margaret
Waddell, Hugh
Waddell, Marion
Waddell, Walter
Waddell, Walter Young
Wallace, Jock
Wilson, William
Gray, John
Orr, Grace
Orr, Thomas
Orr, William
Stark, Grace
Stein, Jock
Waddell, Grace
Waddell, Hugh jr.
Waddell, Marion sr.
Waddell, Walter jr.
Waddell, William Tweedie Orr
White, Davie

Chapter 7: Eddie Turnbull

Cowan, Janet
Cowan, Lily
Doylie, Mary
Easton, Agnes Wilson
Easton, Alexander
Easton, George
Easton, George
Hunter, Robert
Jenkins, Agnes Easton
Jenkins, Alexander
Jenkins, Alexander jr
Jenkins, Alexander sr
Jenkins, Elizabeth
Jenkins, Elizabeth jr
Jenkins, James
Jenkins, Janet
Jenkins, John
Jenkins, Robert
Johnstone, Bobby
Oliver, John
Ormond, Willie
Park, Rev William
Petrie, Rod
Reilly, Lawrie
Smith, Gordon
Turnbull, Agnes Easton
Turnbull, Alexander Jenkins
Turnbull, Edward Hunter
Turnbull, George
Turnbull, Henry
Turnbull, James
Turnbull, James
Turnbull, Mary
Turnbull, Mary Doylie
Turnbull, Thomas
Turnbull, William
Turner, Edward
Turner, Elizabeth
Turner, William
Watt, Rev Alexander K

Chapter 8: Willie Ormond

Esplin, David
Esplin, John
Esplin, Margaret
Esplin, William
Gottier, Elizabeth B
Johnstone, Mary
Kerr, Elizabeth
McCallum, Gilbert
McCallum, Janet
McLachlan, Matilda
McMeechan, Charles
McMeechan, Mary Turner
McNaughton, Jessie
McNaughton, John
McNaughton, Margraet
McNaughton, William
Morrison, Margaret
Orchison, Susan
Ormond, Alexander
Ormond, Bert
Ormond, Charles
Ormond, Gibby
Ormond, Robert
Ormond, Robert Doniston
Ormond, William Esplin
Ormond, William Esplin sr
Palmer, Agnes
Roy, Alexander
Turnbull, Eddie
Wallace, Rev James
Wright, Rev P

Chapter 9: Tommy Docherty

Campbell, Rev Robert
Docherty, Daniel
Docherty, John
Docherty, Neil
Docherty, Neil sr
Docherty, Thomas Henderson
Docherty, Thomas Henderson sr
Fleming, Catherine
Frame, Georgina Neillie
Frame, James
Henderson, Jane
Henderson, Thomas
Hogan, Jimmy
McGahan, John
McLaren, Catherine
McLaren, Daniel
McLaren, Daniel sr
McLaren, Marion
McLaren, Neil
Neillie, Mary
Newlands, Maggie
O'Farrell, Frank
Paterson, Ann
Paul, Elizabeth
Stevenson, John
Stevenson,Cath
Watson, Agnes
Watson, Rev David

Chapter 10: Ally MacLeod

Cameron, Andy
Coltart, Agnes Jane
Farquhar, Rev John L
Gemmill, Archie
Good, Grace
Hope, Christina
Hope, James
Hope, John
Hope, Robert
Horn, Ann
MacLeod, Alexander Reid
MacLeod, Jean
MacLeod, Susan
MacLeod, Thomas Kerr
Petrie, Susan
Reid, Grace
Smith, Edward
Smith, Janet
Smith, Robert
Souness, Graeme
Waddell, Rev P Hately
Collie, Georgina Caie
Erskine, John
Galbraith, Annie
Gibson, Grace
Hope, Agnes
Hope, David
Hope, Jean
Hope, Margaret
Hope, William
Johnstone, William
MacLeod, Duncan
MacLeod, Margaret
MacLeod, Thomas
MacLeod, William Hay
Reid, Alexander
Reid, Janet
Smith, Jane Ann
Smith, John
Smith, Teen Hope
Sturrock, Rev George

Chapter 11: Jock Wallace

Bridges, Nellie
Churchill, Winston
Cleghorn, Janet Dickson
Cochrane, Annie
Cochrane, Wilhelmina
Cruyff, Johan
Dalziel, Martha Jane
Donaldson, Catherine Sinclair Veitch
Donaldson, John
Donaldson, Robert Gardner
Ferguson, Alex
Fleming, Rev J A
Gourlay, John
Greig, John
McGettigan, Fr Patrick
McLean, Jim
Naples, Frances
Sinclair, Catherine
Veitch, Daniel
Veitch, Georgina Sinclair
Veitch, James
Veitch, Wilhelmina Anderson
Waddell, Willie
Wallace, David
Wallace, Jamesina Bridges
Wallace, Janet McAllister
Wallace, John
Wallace, John Martin
Wallace, John Martin Bokas
Wallace, John sr
Wallace, Peter
Wallace, Susan

Chapter 12: Jim McLean

Barclay, Rev Alexander
Brannan, James
Chapman, Pastor Robert
Gwynne, Mary
Hamilton, David
Hamilton, Elizabeth
Marshall, Elizabeth
Marshall, William
McCormick, Alexander
Mclean, James
McLean, Janet
McLean, Sarah
McLean, Thomas sr
McLean, William
McLean, Willie
Smith, Annie
Yuille, Annie Smith
Yuille, Mary Gwynne
Yuille, William
Brannan, Bridget
Brannan, Mary
Cook, Agnes
Hamilton, Barbara
Hamilton, David sr
Higgins, Catherine
Marshall, Mary
McCombs, Janet
McCormick, Isabella Davidson
McLean, James Yuille
McLean, Margaret Docherty
McLean, Thomas
McLean, Tommy
McLean, William sr
Pate, John
Stein, Jock
Yuille, James
Yuille, Robert

Chapter 13: Craig Brown

Brown, Hugh Craig
Brown, James
Brown, James Craig
Brown, James Lamont
Brown, Margaret Smith
Brown, Robert Stevenson
Caldow, Margaret Fleming
Caldow, Mary Gibson
Caldow, Robert
Caldow, Robert Fleming
Caldow, William
Craig, Jeanie
Craig, Martha Lamont
Fleming, Margaret
Gibson, Bessie
Gibson, John
Gibson, Mary Bethel
Gilmour, Jessie Baird
Hitler, Adolf
Jeffrey, Rev George Johnstone
McGee, Archie
McGee, Jimmy
Millar, Alexander
Reid, Rev James
Roxburgh, Andy
Shankly, Bill
Shankly, Bob
Smith, David L
Thomson, Rev Robert Nicholson
Vogts, Berti
Walker, Ernie

Chapter 14: Walter Smith

Alston, Rev Andrew
Brown, Hugh
Brown, Margaret
Burns, George
Campbell, Agnes sr
Craig, Elizabeth
Douglas, Rev Mr
Eadie, John
Ferguson, Alex
Knox, Archie
McCabe, Lawrence
McGhie, Jane
McGhie, Thomas
Pryde, Rev Thomas
Rogerson, Andrew
Rogerson, Elizabeth Burns
Rogerson, James sr
Rogerson, Jane sr
Rogerson, John sr
Rogerson, William
Scoular, Margaret
Smith, Andrew
Smith, James
Smith, Jean
Smith, John
Smith, John sr
Smith, Margaret
Smith, Robert
Smith, Walter Ferguson sr
Brown, Elizabeth
Brown, Maggie
Burns, Elizabeth
Campbell, Agnes
Campbell, John
Douglas, Elizabeth
Dryden, Helen
Eadie, Margaret
Gallacher, Helen
McCabe, Anna
McCoist, Ally
McGhie, Jemima
McLean, Jim
Rodger, Rev J Lyle
Rogerson, Elizabeth
Rogerson, James
Rogerson, Jane
Rogerson, John
Rogerson, Rachel
Russell, Thomas
Smith, Agnes
Smith, Ann C
Smith, Janet
Smith, Jean jr
Smith, John Robert
Smith, Lawrence
Smith, Mary
Smith, Walter Ferguson
Souness, Graeme

Spiers, Hugh
Spiers, Mary
Vogts, Berti
Wallace, Margaret
Wilson, Davie
Wright, Alex

Chapter 15: Graeme Souness

Brown, Adam
Brown, Alex
Brown, Margaret
Butcher, Terry
Charlton, Jack
Dalglish, Kenny
Davidson, Rev Thomas
Dudgeon, Agnes
Edgar, Elizabeth Jane Johnston
Edmond, Marion
Ferguson, Alex
Ferguson, Alexander
Ferguson, Elizabeth Carrie
Ferguson, John
Ferguson, Margaret
Ferguson, William
Francis, Trevor
Hamilton, Rev J E
Hansen, Alan
Keddie, Mary
Kilpatrick, Grace
Macaulay, Rev George
McColl, Henry M
McGinnes, Williamina Thomson
Mearns, Catherine
Murdoch, Bobby
Nicholson, Bill
Park, Rev James
Porteous, Rev Thomas
Simpson, Elizabeth Jane Brack
Simpson, James
Souness, Adam
Souness, Adam sr
Souness, Annie
Souness, Graeme James
Souness, James
Souness, James Simpson
Souness, Thomas
Souness, Thomas sr
Stirling, Elizabeth
Wallace, Jock
Watt, James
Watt, Jemima
Wilkins, Ray
Woods, Chris

Chapter 16: Gordon Strachan

Brown, Craig
Brown, Margaret
Campbell, Colin
Carse, Catherine Livingstone
Carse, David Wright
Carse, Isobel
Cox, Rev B A
Donoghue, Catherine
Donoghue, Joseph
Duncan, Jane
Fleming, Dr Robert A
Kerr, Elizabeth
Lamb, Alexander Lundie
Lamb, Benjamin Bellinger Macpherson
Lamb, Charles James
Lamb, George
Lamb, George Fotheringham
Lamb, Margaret Isabella
Lamb, Mary Ann Bellinger
Lamb, Thomas
Lamb, Thomas Henry
Lavin, Mary Ann
Levein, Craig
Lundie, Agnes
McLeish, Alex
Morrison, Rev Archibald
Murdoch, Rev Alex D
Nichol, J S
O'Neill, Martin
Rafferty, Bridget
Rafferty, Michael
Slimman, Agnes
Slimman, Charles
Slimman, Mary
Stewart, Dr Ian S
Strachan, Alexander
Strachan, Gordon David
Strachan, James Gordon
Tripp, June
Turnbull, Eddie

By the Same Author

Writing as Derek Beaugarde

About the author

Derek Niven is a pseudonym of the author John McGee, a member of ASGRA, for his factual and genealogical books and Derek Beaugarde for his fictional science fiction books. John McGee was born in 1956 at Corkerhill railway village in Glasgow. He attended Mosspark Primary and Allan Glen's schools. The late actor Sir Dirk Bogarde spent three years at Allan Glen's when he was a pupil named Derek Niven van den Bogaerde, thus the observant reader will readily be able to discern the origin of the Two Dereks. After spending 34 years in the rail industry in train planning and accounting he retired in 2007. In 2012 the idea for his science fiction novel first emerged and led to 2084 The End of Days © Derek Beaugarde 2016. In the years leading up to 2084 seven men and women across the globe find themselves drawn together in order to fight for survival against the ultimate global disaster – Armageddon! 2084 The End of Days is their story and mankind's destiny. The following year he published Pride of the Lions: the untold story of the men and women who made the Lisbon Lions © Derek Niven 2017.

Lightning Source UK Ltd.
Milton Keynes UK
UKHW021111071118
331911UK00005B/205/P